Financial *Peace*

REVISITED

Dave Ramsey

Financial Peace

REVISITED

WITH THOUGHTS BY

Sharon Ramsey

VIKING

VIKING
Published by the Penguin Group
Penguin Putnam, Inc., 375 Hudson Street,
New York, New York 10014, U.S.A.
Penguin Books Ltd, 80 Strand, London WC2R 0RL, England
Penguin Books Australia Ltd, 250 Camberwell Road, Camberwell, Victoria 3124, Australia
Penguin Books Canada Ltd, 10 Alcorn Avenue,
Toronto, Ontario, Canada M4V 3B2
Penguin Books India (P) Ltd, 11 Community Centre,
Panchsheel Park, New Delhi - 110 017, India
Penguin Books (N.Z.) Ltd, Cnr Rosedale and Airborne Roads, Albany, Auckland, New Zealand
Penguin Books (South Africa) (Pty) Ltd, 24 Sturdee Avenue, Rosebank,
Johannesburg 2196, South Africa

Penguin Books Ltd, Registered Offices:
Harmondsworth, Middlesex, England

This edition published in 2003 by Viking Penguin,
a member of Penguin Putnam, Inc.

21 23 25 27 29 30 28 26 24 22

LIBRARY OF CONGRESS CATALOGING-IN-PUBLICATION DATA
Ramsey, Dave.
Financial peace revisited / Dave Ramsey ; with thoughts by Sharon Ramsey.
p. cm.
Includes bibliographical references.
ISBN 0-670-03208-5
1. Finance, Personal. 2. Finance, Personal—Religious aspects—Christianity.
I. Ramsey, Sharon. II. Title.
HG179 .R3153 2003
332.024—dc21 2002035830

This book is printed on acid-free paper. ♾

Printed in China

To my wonderful wife, Sharon, who stuck it out while I learned all these lessons the hard way.

She has embodied the truth that real love is commitment, even when it is not fun.

Thank you, honey.

I love you.

Preface

THE STORY OF *Financial Peace* is both my own story—what happened to me and to my family when I got caught up to my eyeballs in debt—and the story of a book that has grown into a phenomenon.

As you'll learn in the pages that follow, I was a young hotshot in real estate in my hometown of Nashville, Tennessee. In the mid-eighties, I was among the first people in the Nashville area to go down, to lose everything. By the time I made it through and was getting back on my feet, a lot of my business associates and friends were being hit by the recession and the crash in real estate. People started coming to me and asking: How'd you do it, Dave? How did you keep your marriage together? How did you put your financial house back together? I started talking to my friends. Then I began counseling couples at my church. After a time, I was offering private financial counseling services—most of which amounted to helping people through their own bankruptcies.

I was helping people, people in emotional pain and financial distress. And despite having learned the hard way, the lessons I was teaching people seemed so easy. Yet I began to realize that most of us don't have the skills to help ourselves because of the way we as Americans are taught and seduced into buying "stuff"—cars, houses, Rolex watches, designer clothing, and on and on. The people I counseled and the groups I spoke to kept asking me for materials to help them implement this system that I was teaching them—the Financial Peace plan.

Finally I decided I'd try to write a book. So I sat down at the computer in my new "office" in the middle of our living room and began writing. When I was done with the manuscript, I showed it to seventeen friends, some of whom were experts in financial matters, and two professional editors. After I got all of their opinions and rewrote the book nineteen times, a local artist designed the cover. I decided it was time to go to press and came to the conclusion that I should print 1,000 copies. It cost me an arm and a leg, I can tell you—and I wasn't quite sure how I was going to sell them, either. By the time I had those thousand books, I knew that the writing had helped me to deal with some of my own wounds from my experiences with debt and bankruptcy and that I had something to say, to teach, and a new mission in life. That was in 1992. I gave most of the first thousand copies of *Financial Peace* away, but kept being asked to teach and to speak and was actually managing to sell a few!

Then there was another bankruptcy. Not my own. It was the local radio station, WWTN-FM in Nashville. It was in distress, filing for Chapter 11, and one of its talk-show hosts quit because he wasn't getting paid. When I heard, I went down to WWTN and offered them a deal. I'd take a time slot for a month at no pay and do a show about money and finances. I thought it'd be fun, maybe. I thought it would help to get my *Financial Peace* message out and, as one of my friends said, maybe I'd "sell a few copies of that dumb ole book" of mine. "The Money Game" went on the air in 1992 and has been on ever since.

It is fun, but it's even more satisfying to help people every day of the week with their money problems and to relieve them of the stress and distress they feel as a result. And we did sell books, some 30,000 of that first edition of *Financial Peace.*

Then in 1995, WWTN was bought by Gaylord Entertainment. You know them—they own the Grand Ole Opry and The Nashville Network among others. They came into WWTN, fixed the tower so we were finally broadcasting at its full 100,000-watt capacity, and began promoting our show. As they geared up, it became clear that this was an opportunity to spread the *Financial Peace* message even further. So I decided to rewrite the book using the lessons I'd learned from the show's listeners and callers, from the questions I got asked by people who came to my seminars, from the new things I had figured out about money in the three intervening years. I also asked my wife, Sharon, to write something in each chapter of the book—she has shared all the pain and the joy of our experiences with financial distress and financial peace so I wanted my readers to hear from her too. Sharon's thoughts turned out to be one of the most popular features of the book.

The new edition of *Financial Peace* hit the stores in September 1995—at the same time that Gaylord's marketing of "The Money Game" hit Nashville. As people got to know the billboards around the Nashville area, they tuned in. The ratings soared—and so did sales of the book. At the end of the year we'd sold some 50,000 copies, with sales growing each week. Six months after that we were up to 120,000 copies. The book became the number-one seller in middle Tennessee for 1995—we beat the big boys!

By mid-1996 we began syndicating the radio show and changed the name to *The Dave Ramsey Show*. You can now hear us on hundreds of radio stations with more than a million listeners daily. We are one of the most listened to talk-radio shows on the Internet and our class Financial Peace University has exploded with over 2,000 locations. As all this was happening Jane von Mehren and another lady with Viking Penguin made me a wonderful offer to take this book national in a way we could only imagine. With over 750,000 copies of *Financial Peace* in print and three new books, we have now sold more than one million books together.

Financial Peace Revisited has tons of new material and totally updated statistics and insights from the original. Our journey to this point has been very tough and very fulfilling. As I travel the nation doing live events and book signings I have met thousands of people who have used the information in this book to completely change their lives: paying off debt, saving money, changing their marriages. I have now heard stories of untold numbers of lives touched and hope restored. That is what *Financial Peace* is about—hope.

Prologue

THE SPEAKER ASKED the people to raise the envelope containing their bills over their heads and to pray for their financial predicaments. With a twinkle in his eye, he said for those with boxes to be careful not to strain their backs. He then prayed over their bills, asking God to remove the bondage that these financial predicaments had brought to their lives. Then came the most significant part.

After the prayer, he asked everyone—from the distinguished businessman to the society lady—everyone—to make the noise that they will make the day that they are no longer in debt or are completely cleared of their financial predicament. I heard a roar and a celebration come from those one thousand people that would rival the Super Bowl. People of every area of life were celebrating the mere thought of being financially free. It was like few expressions of joy I have ever witnessed. Just when I thought they were slowing and going to quiet down, another wave of celebration crossed the hall.

I had been sitting in a meeting on personal finance held in a local church. This experience helped reiterate to me the amount of pain we, the American people, have regarding our personal finances. I had been researching and living this book for four years at that point. What I witnessed was an emotional reminder to me that we as a people have to get a handle on our finances. *It is time.* It is time we started controlling our money, instead of money—or the lack of money—controlling us! The scene I witnessed that night was merely a reflection of what I have seen as a paralyzing cancer that is rampant in our country.

You may think that this was merely some religious emotionalism. However, my counseling experience with thousands of people in financial crises tells me that a huge percentage, even a scary percentage, of the American public at large would throw an unprecedented nationwide celebration if they could simply get control of their finances.

And there is a way. . . .

Acknowledgments

When you have lived as much of this material as we have, writing this was somewhat like birthing a child. I wish to thank all those people who have inspired me through the task of a first book:

To my friends and pastors at Christ Church Nashville, thank you for being my editors, readers, and examples of how we are all supposed to walk before the Lord.

To my parents, whose entrepreneurial spirit has always told me to get up and go on.

To my Lord Jesus, for the power and mercy that You have shown in my life and most of all for Your grace without which I would be lost.

Contents

Financial Peace

REVISITED

CHAPTER ONE

The Beginning . . . a Very Good Place to Start

AS I STOOD PUTTING GAS in my Jaguar, the cold damp January wind chilled me and seemed to dampen my spirits even more. I hoped the attendant inside would not run a telephone check on my gold card. If he did, they probably would turn me down. Then where would I be?

"This is ridiculous," I murmured. "Only in America could you drive a Jaguar and not have the money to put gas in it." I wondered where the arrogant young man from a few years ago was. There I stood in the cold, a man in my twenties, knowing I was in the process of losing virtually everything I owned.

It had not always been that way. After college I hit a couple of minor bumps in my career, but I found a niche in foreclosure bargain real estate. With a formal education in finance, a family background in real estate, and a burning desire to succeed, I had a head start on life. As my real estate business grew, everything I touched seemed to turn to gold. I began to collect rental properties, as well as buy and sell bargain properties. I was very good at it and made money quickly. By age twenty-six, I had a rental real estate portfolio worth more than $4 million. I had built a team of people to manage this growing company and everything was moving perfectly.

Or so I thought. My wife and I did all the exotic vacations, drove the top-name autos, and wore only expensive, custom-tailored suits. You may be able to imagine that for a young man of twenty-six, I thought I had it made.

Financial Independence

I had arrived at "financial independence," that mystical place every young entrepreneur wants to reach. If I wanted something, I bought it—no thought required. I had done it honestly, with hard work and intelligence. So what could possibly happen in paradise?

Along with my knack for obtaining bargains, I had another talent. I had an unusual ability to finance everything. If one of my business lines of credit ran low, I would put on my custom suit, get in my Jaguar, and head for the bank. I would make sure to park in front of the manager's window for a big impression. I had my financial statements, corporate strategy, and tax returns all bound for presentation. All this pomp and circumstance, combined with the fact that my "deals" always worked and enamored the bankers, and they loved to lend me money.

We had every type of personal line of credit, business lines of credit, and equity lines of credit—and let's not forget those wonderful gold and platinum cards.

If a banker would dare to indicate I might have too much debt, I would hunt another source. I have taken a $20,000 draw on a line of credit in a cashier's check, walked out of that bank, and into another. With all the "presentation" explained above and a $20,000 cashier's check, I would "establish a new relationship." Which meant I would deposit my borrowed cash into their bank, promise to be a customer, and in return they would give me a new $100,000 line of credit plus every platinum card and personal line of credit they had.

The sarcastic way that I am explaining this to you almost makes the process seem immoral. However, we were making money, and we had a bright future, so the banks wanted customers like us.

All Good Things Come to an End

Then it happened. Our largest lender was sold to a larger bank. Neither pomp and circumstance nor my name meant anything to the new upper management. Also, the 1986 tax act began to have its negative impact on real estate so all the banks began to get worried. Upper management decided to "trim back" on real estate lending. Most of our borrowing was in short-term notes because we resold most of our property for profit. Because we had "open lines of credit" and short-term notes, the banks had the right to call (or demand that we pay) most of our debt within ninety days. And *that* is just what they did. The new management called all my notes.

I had ninety days to find $1.2 million. I paid virtually all of it, but doing so destroyed my business. That action started a chain reaction that ended in my losing everything but my home and the clothes on my back.

I remember the strain on my marriage. I remember the mornings standing in the shower with the water scalding my face and crying like a baby. I remember the sheriff serving the lawsuit papers for default on notes. I remember thinking of suicide, knowing I had a $1 million life insurance policy that would provide for my family better than I was doing. It took three and a half years for paradise to completely unravel and for me to end up broke.

From the nightmare and emotional pain, however, was born an idea—the idea of counseling the average consumer through debt problems. I found that the foreclosure experience I had, combined with my personal experience with financial pain, was a foundation for opening a company to counsel consumers. I attended any and every workshop or seminar available and devoured every book I could find on consumer financial problems.

I have that company and have dealt with several thousand cases of consumer counseling on financial crisis. The base of knowledge from that experience and my personal pain are the source for this material.

Enough Pain Already!

Having lived through that trepidation, having sat with countless others while they lived through the same horrors of financial stress, and having watched more than 10,000 foreclosures come across my desk in ten years, I have had enough! It is time we Americans get a handle on our finances. We have been Gomer Pyle-ing it through our lives long enough. Down South we call this ridiculous walk down apathy lane in a Valium state of mind "ditty bopping along."

I believe it is time for the typical American family to get out of financial bondage. I also believe that they are ready. Furthermore, I believe that through knowledge and discipline *financial peace* is possible for us—all of us.

At the end of each chapter my wife, Sharon, will offer her insights and comments on the material presented there. Achieving financial peace would have been impossible without her.

Thoughts from Sharon . . .

I remember that sunny summer afternoon when Dave called and told me that nothing else could be done. It was over. We had to declare bankruptcy.

What would we do now? *I wondered. I had such an empty feeling. I felt that the whole world was crashing in on us. Now everybody was going to know our secret. Everybody would look at us funny. What would our family and friends think?*

Would we be able to take nice vacations? Would the children still be able to dress nicely and participate in the same activities? What was going to happen to us?

Question after question raced through my mind. But I didn't have the answers. I began to think, well, maybe I spent too much on furniture. Or maybe I bought too many clothes. What did I do to cause this mess? I was scared—no, I was terrified.

That day I asked the Lord for help. I realized that Dave and I needed more than just money. We needed peace and security so that everything would be okay. I have seen this valley we were in turn into an opportunity to share with others about the financial burden we had gotten ourselves into.

There is hope. As a wife and mother, I knew that I couldn't give up.

There were times I had to be there for Dave just as he was for me. We had to encourage one another many times. I realized that it wasn't going to be easy.

But I knew we were just in a valley and that on the other side there was a mountain and sunshine.

CHAPTER TWO

Enough of Anything Is Too Much

THE AMERICAN CONSUMER is facing dire financial straits. The story outlined for you in the previous chapter and the thousands of families I have counseled lead me to that conclusion. After witnessing national trends and gathering information from personal observation over the past twenty years, I am disturbed by the direction our management of money has taken.

Our nation's financial situation, with record budget deficits and bank failures, is deplorable. However, the nation's situation is only a reflection of our own personal inability to "just say no" to ourselves. Our failure to get control of financial matters in our personal lives will have to be rectified before we can demand accountability from elected officials. Our spoiled Congress is only a reflection of our spoiled selves. The good of our country is overlooked so our pet special-interest groups can be served, just like the good of the family is often overlooked so Dad or Mom can have that special trinket they must possess.

Dessert Before Dinner

As a people we have forgotten how to delay pleasure. We are living in a society that microwaves everything. We must have it, and we must have it now! As Brian Tracy, a well-known motivational speaker, says, "We are being taught by everything around us to have *dessert before dinner.*" Now we are paying for our lack of knowledge and discipline.

The statistics of financial failure show clearly that this decline is a fact. These statistics do not reveal cycles but rather, more alarmingly, show steady decline. These statistics do not show any attributable correlation with inflation, unemployment, recession, or any national trend except the rise in personal debt. Larry Burkett of Christian Financial Concepts says that in 1929 only 2 percent of American homes had a mortgage and by 1962 only 2 percent *didn't* have mortgages.[1]

We must not be misled into believing that these problems are faced only by large companies or deadbeats. On the contrary, these are typical American families with two kids, a dog, and dinner every night. I have met with these families and they are just regular folks. Their situation just got out of control.

The Consumer Reports Money Book states that the typical household has $38,000 in debt and that total consumer debt has almost tripled just since 1980. In 1980 the total consumer debt was $1.3 trillion, and now it is beyond the incredible figure of $3.3 trillion—in just a few short years.[2] A recent survey conducted by Consolidated Credit Counseling Services found that 71 percent of Americans say debts are making their home lives unhappy.[3] A recent study in *The Wall Street Journal* states that 70 percent of the American public lives from paycheck to paycheck.[4] Interestingly, a Marist Institute poll published right after that *Wall Street Journal* article stated that 55 percent of Americans "always" or "sometimes" worry about their money.[5] If 70 percent are broke and only 55 percent are worried, I guess the other 15 percent are asleep.

The Federal Reserve says mortgage debt has more than doubled since the early nineties.[6] Foreclosure has become a way of life in America with tall grass and hanging gutters in virtually every neighborhood. Foreclosures have increased 200 percent since 1980 with more than 600,000 homes lost in 2001 alone.[7] The American Bankruptcy Institute says that in 1980 there were just more than 500,000 bankruptcies filed and by last year almost 1,500,000 were filed with new records set almost every year in between.[8] It is getting ugly. Seventy-one percent of the bankruptcies are Chapter 7, which is the "total" bankruptcy where you lose everything, but 95 percent of those cases were "no asset" cases.[9] That means they had no assets to lose by the time they got to bankruptcy.

As a matter of fact, a recent study done on the typical bankruptcy by the University of Texas in conjunction with the University of Pennsylvania confirms this. Published in the *Wall Street Journal,* the study noted that the typical bankruptcy was not a guy under a bridge or a real estate high roller but rather "well-educated, middle class baby boomers with big time credit card debt."[10]

The Times They Are A-Changin'

In the 1950s you seldom would have heard of a person filing bankruptcy, being foreclosed on, or having his wages garnisheed for nonpayment of debt. Now, if you live in a middle-income neighborhood, out of your closest one hundred neighbors there is at least one house empty from foreclosure, plus one foreclosure under way, and four to seven of your neighbors are more than three months behind on their house payment. In some areas these numbers are double. The generation of adults that started housekeeping in the 1930s and 1940s would be appalled at their grandchildren's lack of financial responsibility.

Since the Civil War we have seen a steady change in the way we Americans handle our money. As a boy in the 1850s, prior to the Civil War, my great-great-grandfather lived in Indiana. In his memoirs he mentions a family who owned a neighboring farm. This family got the fever to move West but couldn't because, unlike most anyone else in the county, they owed money on their farm. The language he used to discuss this mortgage gave insight into the attitude of the day regarding debt. He gave the impression that one should pity this family as if they had cancer or view them as sinners who had some skeleton in their closet. This view of debt is completely foreign to us today. Astonishingly, the mortgage in question was only five dollars!

The generation of people who set up housekeeping in the 1930s and 1940s was scarred by the Great Depression. Those folks would borrow very seldom, and they lived under their means. They would be shocked by the way most families live today.

The family of the 1950s and early 1960s began borrowing in order to buy a home, because "How in the world could you expect a young couple to pay $13,500 cash for a house?" (Incidentally, that same house in most cities is now worth over $100,000.) This family would borrow on very little else except a house because the Depression-era mentality of their parents had partially been passed on to them.

The family of the late 1960s and 1970s, however, began to borrow in order to purchase homes and automobiles and a few other items. Credit cards became popular during this time as a result of the first aggressive marketing of credit. For the first time ever, Americans were sold on the idea of borrowing. Financial institutions began to develop "financial products," meaning an array of different ways that they would lend us money. You will see later the wealth that these companies have attained as the result of selling America on debt. Jupiter Media's study says that there are 15.4 billion credit advertising impressions on the American public every three months![11]

The seventies, eighties, nineties, and the new millennium have seen lending and borrowing at an all-time high in modern history. We want it all, and we can borrow to get it all, before we can afford it all. Over the last forty years we have gradually become a nation of *consumers*, instead of the nation of *producers* we used to be.

Stuff

We must have everything *now*, and we want only the best. We cannot be content to have just a DVD. We must have one that tells the time in Japan while simultaneously recording soap operas in Afghanistan three weeks from now! We cannot be content to own a refrigerator to keep food from rotting; we must have one that talks and makes sandwiches at halftime. Don't get me wrong; I am not criticizing owning nice things because I own "stuff." However, we have stressed our family budgets and often crashed ourselves by buying all this "stuff" before we can really afford it.

Our businesses have followed the same general change in philosophy. Businesses used to believe in having high cash reserves, but now most are run on a shoestring, with no provision for the cycles that *do* come. Businesses now believe in joint ventures, leveraged buyouts (which simply means the entire purchase is on borrowed funds, which usually strains the company to an unhealthy position), and the heavy use of capital markets of all kinds. Consequently, in the last few years we have seen the highest rate of business failure ever. The volatility brought on by business failures has rippled through every part of our lives, spreading insecurity, fear, and actual financial, spiritual, and emotional damage.

The American family has especially felt the effects of these changes in our financial philosophy. The very core of the family is dramatically affected by this overbuying, which creates overborrowing. Most marriages that fail list financial problems as a contributing factor, if not the main reason for the failure. Marriages of twenty-five years or more are frequently destroyed by foreclosure or bankruptcy. The "stuff" must have owned them, instead of their owning the "stuff."

Our entire nation is in financial stress at the individual level, at the city and state level, and at the national level. Are you depressed yet? I hope so. I intend for this chapter not to make you feel guilty or simply to leave you hopeless, but instead to get you mad. I want you mad enough to change your life and mad enough to change your children's lives—and maybe even mad enough to change your city or your country.

Mad Is Not the Word for It

I have had enough! Enough living in bondage to "stuff." Enough of having a bank collector, credit card collector, or mortgage company call and ruin my evening with those collection calls. I finally got sick and tired of it! And when I got sick and tired of being sick and tired, I decided to learn something about money, how it works—how it *really* works—and how to work it. I decided to learn the things not taught in college finance class. I decided after losing virtually everything I owned that I was tired of living in stress due to money or the lack of money.

After counseling for several years, I am still mad. I am tired of seeing my friends divorce over money problems. I am tired of having grown men and women in my office with thoughts of suicide because they stand to lose everything they own. I am tired of seeing single moms work seventy-hour weeks just to make a living and put food on the table. I am tired of watching our Congress and president pass more trillion-dollar deficits.

Is there hope? Absolutely, but we must shift our view of "stuff" and money, and we have to learn how to handle both. I see dramatic things happen to people who apply simple and forgotten principles to all areas of their life. You too can turn your personal financial problems and challenges into opportunities in just a few weeks. You can redirect your entire life within just a short period of time. I am even optimistic that our nation can and will be saved by a return to simple, basic principles that have been taught and lived since Old Testament times.

If you need more peace in your financial life, finish this book. As I said in the preface, there is a way. . . .

Thoughts from Sharon . . .

We all love stuff—men, women, and children, but probably women more so! Let's face it: women love to shop.

We had a garage sale last year, and I thought to myself, why do we have so much stuff? Do we really need all of this? If so, then why am I trying to sell it all? Well, I believe the answer to those questions is because at one time we thought we needed it.

Yes, I have to admit it was very hard for me to be content with what I had. Fifty more times I would say, "If I could only have . . ." Dave's answer would always be, "Then you would want more." It's always a cycle—I want, I want, I want. I hear it every time we go to a special store with the children, and I am sure you have too.

Over the years it has been hard to be content. I am realizing now that it really doesn't matter. I have so much compared to so many others in other countries, states, and towns. I am blessed with "other" types of stuff. Each day I look at my husband, two daughters, and son. I know that I am blessed. I'm thankful for the house I have, the car I drive, and the food I eat. At the end of each day I realize again that I'm content and blessed with all my "stuff."

CHAPTER THREE

The Basics (a Foundation)

WE AMERICANS, with all our bad habits, are not necessarily bad people. The people who have come to me for crisis financial counseling, as well as those who come to me with property in foreclosure, are not evil people. They are not scammers or schemers who got caught and are going to jail as soon as they lose their homes. These people in trouble are in your family. They work with you, they live on your street, and sometimes they are you. I have seldom met anyone who set out with a plan to defraud creditors or steal money by borrowing and not paying it back. Then, if not because of their lack of morals, what gets people in trouble?

As a culture we are ignorant of what money is and how to handle it. Ignorance is not lack of intelligence; it is lack of knowledge on a particular subject. If I were put in a chemistry lab, I would probably blow up something. But

I am not unintelligent. I am ignorant of chemistry. If you needed brain surgery I doubt you would call me, not because I am unintelligent, but because I am ignorant of brain surgery and its processes.

How Can This Be?

It is almost impossible to get out of high school today without knowing what an amoeba is—now there is a really valuable piece of information—but few high school seniors can keep a checkbook balanced. They are taught virtually nothing about the real world of money. I am not talking about money on Wall Street. I am talking about money on your street. We are not taught basic principles of managing and making financial decisions for our own family.

Consequently, we come out of high school or even college and set up housekeeping. We don't have knowledge of leases, but we sign one. We don't have knowledge of cars and car financing, but we buy one and sign the loan papers. We don't have knowledge of the implications of credit cards and high interest rates, but we get five preapproved cards in the first two years out of school and we use them. We don't know about the Rule of 78s or prepayment penalties, so we finance our waterbeds, stereos, TVs, and washers and dryers. It was all so innocent and happened so slowly that the monster in the closet was not noticeable.

The Famous Five-Year Mark

After about five years of marriage the average couple begins to feel pinched in the pocketbook. They have little or no savings and start to get scared. They may get scared enough to curb spending for about six months, but then they go back to their old ways and still end up in trouble very quickly. All of this could have been prevented by some basic knowledge.

In my counseling of the "average" couple, I found their problem to be simply a lack of knowledge and discipline. I have found that money has two properties that most people don't acknowledge or understand.

Very Active

First, *money is active.* Finance and money are always moving. Time, interest rates, amounts, cash flows, inflation, and risk all intermingle to create a current that is ever flowing. Whether you choose to impact these currents is irrelevant, they still go on. If you took $10,000 and buried it in the backyard for ten years, will it buy as much when you dig it up as it will now? Obviously not. We must learn that the current or flow of the mathematical process is always affecting our money. It *never* stops.

Money in this sense is like a beautiful thoroughbred horse—very powerful and always in action, but unless this horse is trained when very young, it will be an out-of-control and dangerous animal when it grows to maturity.

The point is this: You must gain control over your money or the lack of it will forever control you.

If you don't take action continually on your money, it or the lack of it will take action on you. Finance is not passive. It *requires* you to take the initiative to control it.

In his popular book, *The Seven Habits of Highly Effective People,* Dr. Stephen Covey says the number-one habit of highly effective people is that they are proactive. They "happen" to things; things don't "happen" to them.

Amoral—No Morals

Second, *money is amoral.* Money has no morals. That is, it is neither good nor bad. First Timothy 6:10 does not say, "Money is the root of all evil." What it does say is "The *love* of money is the root of all evil." Money in and of itself has no more moral quality than a brick. So just because you are poor does not mean that you are good or spiritually superior; neither does it mean that you are bad or spiritually inferior. On the other hand, having wealth does not mean that you are inherently good or spiritually superior, nor does it mean that you are a crook or a bad person or spiritually inferior. You decide what you are. The way you act through your money or your lack of it will show us whether *you* are good or evil, but the money itself is neither.

Where Is Your Value?

Be careful of a society that assigns value to a person based upon its wrong view of collecting "stuff." Your value as a human being, as a person, is not based on your ability to collect "stuff." If you have jumped on this train of thought, you will be derailed because the first money principle will get you. Money is "active" in the philosophical realm as well. When your priorities get off track, money will take command instantly because of its active principle. I love the old adage "Measure your wealth not by the things you have, but by the things for which you would not take money."

Money is simply a nonentity that must be manipulated. The better we are at manipulating it, the more of it we will control. Until we take this "active" and "amoral" view of money, it will continue to have the upper hand in every part of our lives.

I have developed and absorbed ideas of personal financial control from much experience and study of experts on this subject. I claim little originality in any of these philosophies, but I simply offer a new presentation of these ideas in a different format. Pain is a very permanent teacher, and I have lived through financial disaster and viewed much pain in others. I have drawn from this background to develop a track on which you can run your finances.

Financial peace and *"the peace puppies,"* which I will

introduce in the next chapter, were developed to help you look at where you are and where you want to be. None of these principles will work in the least if *you* don't work *them*, but if you do work them these principles will lead you directly to financial peace.

Do pass go; *do* collect your $200.

Good luck!

Thoughts from Sharon . . .

I remember as a child how fun it was to spend money. Every Saturday my brothers and sisters (mainly sisters) had special chores. When each had been completed, we would be paid a certain allowance. At that time, I didn't really understand the meaning or value of money. I mostly remember watching my piggy bank growing fatter and fatter.

My parents were great parents. I appreciate the upbringing they gave me, but I must admit we weren't taught the concepts of money. As a senior in high school I took a class called general business and loved it. During that class I was taught how to keep a checkbook and saw my first profit and loss sheet.

After going to college for three years, I met Dave. He knew as much about money then as he does now. Here I was spending and wasting so much until he explained to me that money didn't grow on trees. For some reason I began to become stingy with what I had.

After time, maturity, and not having Mom or Dad to refurbish the checking account, I began to understand that every dollar has real value.

CHAPTER FOUR

Understand the Spiritual Aspects of Money

THERE ARE THOSE who believe that finance is merely an exact mathematical science. That is the way it is taught in the universities. In fact, finance is an exact mathematical science—until a human touches it. Personal finance is who you are. The personal, philosophical, and emotional problems and strengths that you have will be reflected in your use of money. If you are very disciplined, you can be a good saver of money. If you are very selfish or self-centered, you will surround yourself with expensive toys that you cannot afford.

The Character of Money

Larry Burkett, a noted author on this subject, says money problems are normally not the real problem but instead are only the symptom of a personal shortfall. My counseling experience confirms Burkett's statement. *Extreme amounts of money or extreme lack of it magnifies character.* A person not committed totally to honesty will tell white lies and sometimes even commit fraud by lying on a loan application when money is tight.

Doug Parsons, in his sermon entitled "A Life Above the Ordinary," tells an interesting story about character. One of the richest and most powerful men in America owned a huge company that employed thousands of people. This gentleman pointed out an up-and-coming low-level manager to his upper-level staff. This young man worked very hard and was very good at his management position. The owner noticed the young man because of his work ethic and talent and commented that someday this young man would be a regional manager long before his time. Sure enough, the young man continued to work hard and was promoted up through the ranks to the point that the next promotion was to be regional manager. When the owner became aware that this promotion was to be made, he decided to fly down and personally give that young man the promotion over lunch.

So the big day arrived and the owner flew in to take the young man to lunch. But as the young man and the owner were going through the cafeteria-style line for lunch, the owner noticed the young man very deliberately hide a one-cent pat of butter under his roll so as not to be charged for it. The lunch went fine—except that no promotion was given—and when the owner returned to his offices he had the young man fired. Not only did the young man miss a several-hundred-thousand-dollar-a-year position, he even lost his job.

A close friend of mine suggested that such an extreme action was a bit severe. Maybe he wanted the warmth of the roll to warm the butter, making it easy to spread. Whatever the other circumstances surrounding the story, the point is that the owner understood that the young man's character flaw of dishonesty would be magnified under pressure and, like a weak spot in an inner tube, would eventually blow out.

What We Do Shows Who We Are

We all have seen people get rich overnight through a lottery or inheritance and, because of their immaturity, blow the entire fortune in the twinkle of an eye. On the other hand, I have seen people who grew as individuals more during financial crises than at any other time in their lives. Martin Luther King said, "The ultimate measure of a man is not where he stands in moments of comfort and convenience, but where he stands at times of challenge and controversy."

Sometimes we see people get wealthy and it magnifies the good character they had within. Steel magnate Andrew Carnegie, a very well-known philanthropist and humanitarian, spent the first half of his life attaining wealth and the last half of his life giving it away. Many of the libraries across our nation were established by his donated funds. Many other famous philanthropists have shown us that their good character was merely magnified by their attainment of wealth. St. Ambrose said, "Just as riches are an impediment to virtue in the wicked, so in the good they are an aid of virtue." Jesus said, "For where your treasure is, there will your heart be also" (Matt. 6:21).

Stuffitis—A Deadly Disease

We Americans like "stuff." We have been called materialistic, self-centered, the "me" generation. I have never liked being accused of being materialistic, but admittedly I do like good "stuff." I like good cars, expensive food, nice clothes, and very large houses, but I am not materialistic.

I am guilty of having contracted a disease known as "stuffitis," where the bearer has an insatiable desire for only "good stuff." If you have "stuffitis," you might seem materialistic, but the difference is that you will not collect just anything, only the good "stuff." (Please do not confuse "the good stuff" with "the right stuff," which stands for internal courage and quick reactions that a great fighter pilot must have.) I am not the only one that has "stuffitis"; in fact, I see people all the time who have it. There is no cure for this disease, but there are ways to control it, as we will discuss in later chapters.

One of the ways you can spot "stuffitis" in its later stages is when people have gotten confused and have not put money in its proper priority. Exodus 32, when Moses comes down from Mount Sinai after receiving the Ten Commandments, can give us insight. What were the people doing that angered him so? Worshiping a golden calf—"stuffitis." When we forget that our money is not our Creator—that instead we are supposed to create with it—we wreak havoc in our lives. Our forefathers may not have intended this, but they put a reminder on our currency to avoid "stuffitis"—"In God We Trust." Please notice it did not say "In 'Stuff' We Trust." We must keep money and our handling of it in the proper perspective. We must not treat it carelessly, for this collecting of "stuff" is only a game of Monopoly.

Independent of What?

We Americans have identified a concept in the last thirty years—and we all strive for it—of being "financially independent." Independent of what? Can you gain enough money that you never have to worry or be cautious again? Can you gain enough money that you can protect your family from injury or sickness? Can you accumulate enough money to be guaranteed you won't lose everything due to war, famine, or the collapse of financial markets? I have never read about or met anyone who could hoard this much money.

You can be a better manager and gain more control and peace in the handling of finance, but you can never be totally independent as long as you are alive. Money is *active,* and you must keep managing it and moving it no matter how much you attain. You can do well—and I expect you to—in handling your money, and you should try to gain as much as you are able, but this pursuit should not become all-consuming. You must be careful of spending all your energy and time trying to reach "financial independence" because this place is as nonexistent as the god of that golden calf.

The Dirty Word

We have discussed how the strengths and weaknesses in your life will affect your personal finances, but we cannot leave that subject without dealing with one of life's dirtiest words—*discipline*. You will have conflict, worry, shortages, and general lack of fun until you achieve some discipline in the handling of your funds. I am not saying you have to run or live in a financial boot camp, but you must start to think before you sign that check. You must begin today to look at your finances differently from how you have done so before. You must recognize that you must bring your finances totally under your control.

To Give or Not to Give?

The last spiritual aspect you must understand is "farming." No farmer has ever grown a crop unless he planted some seed. Personal growth requires that you give money away. The institutions to which you give will survive if you don't give, but you will have missed an opportunity to benefit. If you feel as if you don't have enough to give, you can start by giving small amounts and by giving of your time. You can give something. Somehow giving reminds us that the world does not revolve around us and that no matter what our financial status is, someone always is in a much worse situation. Good things that cannot be calculated or quantified are set in motion in your life and in your finances when you give; I have seen many couples make the turn toward financial peace simply by adhering to this principle.

You need to plant some seed in self-growth, and you can do this only by giving. I do not totally understand what giving does to the human spirit, but I do know that I meet very few well-balanced, happy, healthy, wealthy people who don't give money away.

You must beware of whom you give to and what they do with the money, however. Being wary does not mean being cynical because there are no perfect institutions. You must be responsible with your giving. John Wesley said, "Make all you can, save all you can, give all you can." Giving helps us keep proper priorities in our lives. It is essential to good money management.

Christians should give tithes to their local church. I will not expand in depth, as that detail is not my purpose here, but instead I will list these Scripture references for those interested:

Genesis 14:18–20
Leviticus 27:30
Numbers 18:26
Deuteronomy 14:22
1 Chronicles 26:20
Malachi 3:7–12
Matthew 23:23
Luke 11:42
Luke 18:12
1 Corinthians 9:7
Hebrews 7:8

"These things you should do . . ."

Just a Matter of Math?

To think that the handling of your personal finances is merely a matter of math control is naive. You must get better control of all aspects of your life. Until you do, the next chapters will have little effect but will instead be neutralized by the other habits in your life. If you drink until it affects your finances, you should get help. If you do drugs or compulsively do *anything* that affects your finances, you should recognize this as a sure sign of an addiction. You must seek counseling because I cannot help you overcome problems at that level, no matter the amount of knowledge presented in the following chapters.

I discovered this little gem at a seminar a few years ago and it applies here. The author is unknown.

I am your constant companion,
I am your greatest helper or your heaviest burden.

I will push you onward or drag you down to failure.
I am at your command.
Half of the tasks that you do you might just as well
turn over to me and I will do them quickly
and correctly.

I am easily managed,
you must merely be firm with me.
Show me exactly how you want something done;
after a few lessons I will do it automatically.
I am the servant of all great people and
alas of all failures as well.
Those who are great I have made great,
those who are failures I have made failures.

I am not a machine, but I work with all the precision
of a machine, plus the intelligence of a person.
Now you may run me for profit or
you may run me for ruin.
It makes no difference to me.
Take me, train me, be firm with me,
and I will lay the world at your feet.
Be easy with me and I will destroy you.

Who am I? I am called Habit.

Please spend five minutes after you finish this chapter in personal reflection. Write down the resolutions—those involving both minor and major change—that you see you must make. Then you can get ready to have some fun and to learn a lot about finally getting control.

Peace Puppies

I would like to introduce you to "peace puppies," which will be developed throughout the balance of the book. (Peace Puppies, meet Reader. Reader, meet Peace Puppies.) These principled puppies must be applied to your life with discipline.

These are great creatures. They are eager to please, love their master, and are inherently loyal. However, if you choose to let them grow up in your life without discipline, they, like any other dog, will become wild and mean. And should you choose not to put these well-disciplined puppies into your life and allow them to grow into mature, loving, and loyal creatures, *let me assure you that you will live a dog's life financially*.

Thoughts from Sharon . . .

Doesn't it make you feel good when someone gives you something? Whether it be a hug from your child or a bouquet of flowers, a gift always makes you smile.

Not only is it fun to receive but it's also fun to give. This is something I had a lot of trouble doing. I felt the only person who needed my money was myself. Until . . .

One Christmas Dave and I, along with the youth from our church, gave gifts to a special family. We acted out the twelve days of Christmas, delivering small gifts to their door unannounced for twelve days prior to Christmas. What joy I received.

During that time, Dave and I did not have a lot of money, but what a blessing. Second Corinthians 9:7 says, "For God loves a cheerful giver."

Giving of our time can also be a great blessing. So much can be given without having to use money. Kind words, hugs, smiles, cards, and phone calls are just a few examples. So many people need to receive these. You can make somebody happy every day by showing others how happy you are—and you will be giving a lot.

Peace Puppies

1. **Avoid "Stuffitis"—**The Worship of "Stuff"
2. **Plant Seeds—**Give Money Away to Worthy Causes

CHAPTER FIVE

Let the Buyer Beware—*Caveat Emptor*

IN THE 1970s when I started in the real estate business, I learned the Latin phrase *caveat emptor,* which means "let the buyer beware." The context was residential real estate in which the seller of the property normally pays the real estate commission. Since the seller is paying the agents, the buyer technically has no representation—so he should "beware." In this age of governmental bureaucracy we assume that as consumers someone or some agency is always watching out for us. We take that for granted, and, in truth, we are reasonably sheltered from actual scams and/or dangerous products.

We Want Your Money

However, we are ignorant as to how much effort, time, energy, and *money* is spent to get our business and thereby our money. While companies spend billions of dollars and hours to sell to us, we sit idly by, getting sold and sold and sold. And many families buy themselves into financial ruin. If you ever are to get control of your financial life you must learn to "just say no" to buying.

Power over Purchase

We must develop a power over purchase—instead of allowing our purchases and the people from whom we make the purchases to have power over us. We must remember that we can *always* spend more than we can make. I once met a man whose annual income in one year increased from $42,000 to $175,000. Both years he spent everything he made. He had no sales resistance, no power over purchase.

Proverbs 14:29 *"He who is impulsive exalts folly."*

Profile of the Enemy

For me to label every honest company or person who wants to sell you something "the enemy" may seem overstated, but in fact it can be the enemy of your financial peace of mind. As consumers, we must quit being so lazy in making purchase decisions—since as a result of our laziness we are often sold goods and services by what are many times juvenile tactics and strategies.

The first area we must consider is personal selling, in which an item is sold to you by another person as a result of one-on-one discussion. This can be as insignificant as

"Do you want fries with your Whopper, sir?" Do we realize that just by adding that statement to every Whopper flopper's training the gross sales of those companies go up millions of dollars annually?

However, the personal selling we are most concerned with involves larger-ticket items—the sale of cars, houses, financial products, furniture, electronics, etc. Any company selling these items that can survive in today's highly competitive business climate has *highly* trained, professional salespeople. Sometimes these salespeople are trained to spout certain pat lines, but even these pat lines are highly developed by upper management. Millions of dollars are spent by companies each year teaching their front-line people how to dress, talk, and walk in order to influence you to buy.

A car salesperson who doesn't have five answers to "I want to think about it" will soon starve. A stereo salesperson who lets you off the property without a sale knows that over 90 percent of the time he has lost that sale. A real estate agent who doesn't make it easy to look past the bright red bedroom and help you through the rigors of finance won't make it. I have sold many a kitchen to a woman and the house just went with it or sold a big basement to a man and the house just went with it.

Good salespeople know a customer who asks a question about the product or service is giving what is called "a buying signal," so the salesperson will just turn on the pitch that much more. For example, a good car salesperson will not just answer yes or no to a question like

"Do you have that car in stock in blue?" Instead he will answer you with "If we do, would you rather finance that on forty-eight or sixty months?"—and when you answer that question you are much closer to buying that car.

This is not a game! It is how these people make a living and if they are not good at persuading you to spend your money on their product or service, they simply starve out of the business. So the sale is very, very important to them. The sale is also important to their company, which also makes a profit. Of course, I am not implying that a good salesperson can make us go into a hypnotic state in which we lose all willpower; I am saying we need to *wake up!* Good salespeople are a reality, and they do have a substantial impact on your purchasing decisions, especially if you are unaware and/or are mentally lazy.

Nothing Down, Nothing a Month

Another way products and services are sold is by offering consumers unbelievable financing. Have you ever heard of "ninety days same as cash" or "no finance charges until January" or "no interest financing"? Did it ever occur to you that in a world so driven by money markets a company offering zero interest with no ulterior motive would soon go broke?

Here is how it really works. First, the product is priced higher to cover the expense, so there is actually no savings—but the story just starts there. Most dealers in this type of approach use a finance company to buy the contract once you execute it. And why would a finance company buy a contract at zero interest? First, the dealer (the furniture or stereo store, etc.) who marked up the item anyway sells the financing contract to the finance company at a discount. The dealer got what he wanted, a sale at a normal profit after the discount to the finance company. So when you come in on the eighty-ninth day of ninety-days-same-as-cash and pay off the finance company, the finance company makes a profit.

Second, and more importantly, over 70 percent of the time *you do not pay him off within the stated period,* according to one of my friends who is a regional manager for a nationally known finance company. Then the finance company gladly begins to charge you interest and puts you on a longer pay plan. And normally when this occurs, you pay over 24 percent interest (if your state allows it) and the contract is on prepaid interest or Rule of 78s, which means you have a huge prepayment penalty. Plus the company will add interest for the original ninety days, which is only "free" if you pay it off. They also typically will sell you overpriced life and disability insurance to pay off their overpriced loan should something happen to your overpriced self. I once met a man who had life insurance on a loan against a rototiller!

This brilliant zero-interest plan now has turned into one of the worst financial decisions ever made because of the total cost of that item. A $1,000 couch at 24 percent for three years with credit life and disability insurance will end up costing at least $1,900.

If this has happened to you, you are in good company. I know a financial planner who bought his VCR this way and even he ended up converting to easy payments. We must learn not to just ask, "How much down and how much a month?" Until you learn this lesson, you will never have financial peace.

I Love TV (Just Kidding)

You also must beware of the subtle sales methods advertisers use on you and your children. Television and radio advertisers understand the power of repetition. Most well-known products are well known because companies spend millions on "brand recognition," positioning their product in your mind as better because of brand. Physiological studies measure your body's reaction to color, label design, and shelf position. The astute company knows what your heart rate, retina reaction, pupil dilation, peripheral vision, protein release, adrenaline release, and many other reactions are to their products and/or their packaging or shelf position. A nationally known real estate franchise at its inception spent over $250,000 studying and developing the color to use on its yard signs just to make sure a person's eye would be more likely to notice that house for sale.

I recently attended an upper management meeting for a nationally known restaurant. Hours were spent discussing minute details, such as the positioning of tables and hostess stations, which would make patrons feel more comfortable. At the same time these details create more "table turns," encouraging people to eat more quickly so that tables are open for other paying customers.

A cold-drink man will fight like mad for the best shelf position in a convenience mart. Many a bread man or candy man or cigarette man might sabotage or even physically fight for a certain display position for his product. This may seem silly or minor to you; however, companies know that proper display or shelf positioning controls impulse-buying decisions and therefore sales may go up or down 500 percent simply with poor versus good positioning. This is not a game to them! Companies constantly develop and implement detailed strategies, and consumers must build some defenses against them. If you don't, you will never get control of your finances.

The final area to consider concerns your body's chemical reaction to a "significant purchase," something that you may not have realized. Documented research identifies certain chemical changes a buyer experiences when making a purchase that is "significant" in terms of its cost. A "significant" purchase is not a candy bar; for most people it is something over $300. As a person moves through the stages of a purchasing decision the heart rate increases, the pupils dilate, and the body releases adrenaline, proteins, hormones, and enzymes.

In short, no matter how calm a person is on the outside, inside he is getting excited. Any one of these chemical changes in excess could be exhibited by a drug addict on a high. Buyers do get a small "rush" from making these purchases. Salespeople call it "the fever" or "buying fever." They know it exists and that everyone is partially influenced by it. Now you know it too, so beware.

The Big Ticket

Several years ago I sold new homes on a building site that sold for $150,000 and up per home. In selling these properties we were aware of this "rush" phenomenon. The average couple who would make a purchase and sign a contract would wake up the next morning, look at each other with fear in their eyes and a knot in their stomachs, and say, "What in the world have we done?" We called this "buyer's remorse," and everyone who has made a big purchase has experienced it. As salespeople we learned to counteract their wanting out of the deal the next day by telling them in advance about "buyer's remorse" and that if they didn't experience it, they were not normal. So the next morning when Joe and Sue would wake up with fear in their hearts, they would remember our explanation and just sigh with relief because they were normal. This technique avoided a lot of contract cancellations. Beware when making a "significant" purchase.

What should you do? First, remember that you are *not helpless;* so quit acting like it. You just need to be aware of this fact when making a "significant" purchase. Second, you must carefully consider your buying motives when making purchasing decisions. Why do you want or think you need this item? Could you live without it? Do you want it for selfish reasons like showing up the neighbors, or is the item of use to you?

Third, purchasing decisions made *slowly* are invariably better decisions. If the purchase is a "significant purchase," you should never buy without waiting overnight. It sounds old-fashioned, not very nineties' advice. Well, so be it. The people of past generations didn't make the bad buying decisions we have made. They didn't have record foreclosures and bankruptcies, which are the norm today.

Finally, you should seek counsel and look carefully for bargains. Two later chapters are devoted entirely to these two ideas.

You must develop power over purchase rather than letting the purchases have power over you. Remember this definition of a rich man—a person who is not *afraid* to ask to see something cheaper.

Thoughts from Sharon . . .

Buying items can be fun. When Dave and I were first married, we wanted everything and we wanted it fast. We shopped lots of furniture stores, clothing stores, and car lots. You name the store, and we could tell you the location.

Dave was always aware of the selling technique. I was still immature in this area but was trying to learn.

Years ago I remember going into both expensive and inexpensive stores and sometimes feeling inadequate. Sometimes I would sort of be nervous because of the selling pressures. It was hard for me to say no. When this would happen, I would say, "Well, I guess I could use it." I knew it was a waste, and I felt used. I had bought something someone else had talked me into—bad, bad, bad. That happened one time too many. I then became wise. I knew this game, and I could play it too. I learned to say no.

So whenever I felt pressured, I would say, "Gosh, my husband would kill me if I came home with this." And the saleslady would look at me kind of funny as I walked away smiling to myself.

Peace Puppies

1. **Avoid "Stuffitis"**—The Worship of "Stuff"
2. **Plant Seeds—**Give Money Away to Worthy Causes
3. Develop Your Own **"Power over Purchase"**

CHAPTER SIX

Career Choice

THE CAREER OR TYPE of work you choose—and whether or not you choose to work at it—can be paramount to your financial peace. Viktor Frankl, author of *Man's Search for Peace*, says that "life is never made unbearable by circumstances, but only by lack of meaning and purpose." Thomas Edison said that "the secret of success is focus of purpose."

Do What Comes Naturally

We will spend well in excess of 100,000 hours of our lives working at our choice of vocation. The sheer math of a per-hour rate makes this decision very important. You must plan your work and then work your plan. Happy and effective people have found a vocation for which they have a natural aptitude and have committed themselves to excellence in that vocation. These are the people who have a vacation for a vocation.

Everyone has some natural talent or aptitude in one or more areas. If you can identify those areas you not only will be happier and perform more successfully in that role, but you will also become better paid for that. Our free-market system pays for performance at some point. When you have a natural talent or aptitude, coupled with desire and experience, the result is productivity plus.

This is such an important financial concept that I recommend detailed aptitude testing if you are not happy and functioning at peak efficiency. These tests are sometimes expensive, but in relative terms if you discover an aptitude for an industry with a salary potential from $75,000 to $100,000 within a few years—and you are making $30,000 now at a job you hate—that is a good deal. The economic change will easily make the testing pay its way, not to mention the self-growth that occurs when you find a vocation that suits your aptitudes.

Go Forth

If you are currently in a vocation that is perfect for you, *it is time to excel*. You must get busy and do the work necessary to excel in what you do. The old saying holds true: if you are going to eat and eat excellently, you must get up, leave the cave, kill something, and drag it home. The boss can't do it for you, the company can't do it for you, and the competition can't do it to you if you have made up your mind to succeed.

This is not some hyped-up vision of success. It just involves hard, hard work at something that comes naturally for you and that will sooner or later catapult you to where you want to be. In most industries you can outwork 80 percent of your cohorts and outsmart (use the knowledge you have) 15 percent of the rest, putting you in the top 5 percent—which always pays very well.

The Two Cycles

If you are good at something, you become more intense, and so you get more creative. Consequently, you accomplish more, so you get paid more. This causes you to enjoy it more, which in turn means you will get better at it. This process is what we call an excellence cycle. If you get caught up in an excellence cycle, you will find that your financial problems will no longer be caused by a low income.

On the other hand, you can get caught in a death cycle. When you finished school, you may have given as little thought to your career as to what clothes to put on that day, and so you entered a field not well suited for you. You may have thought about your direction based on what your parents or your friends thought should be *your* direction, and so you entered a field not well suited for you. A lot of people feel this way, and it takes its toll. An article in the *Los Angeles Times* reports that the risk of heart attack is 33 percent higher on Monday morning.[1] If so, you probably hate what you do, are less intense, and are less creative. As a result, you accomplish less, and you get paid less or you level off. Now you become even more unhappy, which starts the cycle again. You need to get out!

You should start making plans today to get away from your bad situation as soon as possible. Aptitude testing will identify a field that you will enjoy. You will be happier, healthier, and wealthier. One warning is in order, however: *Do not quit your job today!* Do not get all excited and destroy your monthly budget by making a rash decision. You can *begin* the process of discovery and transformation *today*.

Sometimes financial necessity forces you to take an extra job just to provide the basics. Second jobs are a hard thing, but they can make a career transition smoother from a financial perspective. You may have to do what is necessary in the short term to make the long term happen.

The Second Income, or Is It?

Many families today have found it necessary to have two incomes to exist. Many women do very well in careers and find much satisfaction. Other times, however, I have observed in my counseling experience a wife and mother working at something she hates because the bills and her husband require that she "do her part." Is this working mom with two kids making a good income—or is it an economic myth? The following example is of one of my clients. How much is she really earning?

Working Mom—$18,000 Annual Salary

INCOME:	MONTHLY	YEARLY
	1,500	18,000
minus—		
Taxes and payroll deduction	550	6,600
TAKE-HOME PAY	950	11,400
minus—		
More extensive wardrobe	100	1,200
Extra dry cleaning	45	540
Extra mileage depreciates car	50	600
Extra maintenance on car	50	600
Day care for two kids @ $65 ea./wk.	560	6,720
Extra meals out due to fatigue	50	600
REAL NET INCOME	95	1,140

This does not mean that women should not work. If a woman is productive and enjoys what she does, then by all means she should go for it. But women should not let the "me generation" trap them into thinking that the only way to have a reasonable style of living is to work their fingers to the bone, because all they may get is *bony fingers*.

Neither should the "me generation" trick women into thinking that the only place to "be all they can be" is in the workplace. Many highly intelligent, articulate, employable women choose a career in the home, and they should not be shamed for doing so. The so-called politically correct thing to do may not be. Maybe even what appears to be the economically correct thing to do will not be so after serious inquiry.

Get Real; Get Focused

When you find the right field of endeavor for you, you will excel financially only if you work hard and are honest. The same light widely dispersed in a room simply lights the room, but when focused to the size of a pin it becomes a laser. At this point you must do some self-inspection to determine if you are lazy. That may seem to be a strange suggestion, but I have never met a lazy person who thinks he is lazy.

If you take time off and call it a sick day when you are not sick or if you work half-speed when the supervisor is not watching, you are guilty of theft. You steal from the company that supports your family, but worst of all, you steal from yourself and make a statement about who you really are.

It is time we turned the corner on this issue of low productivity. Sadly, in most cases, low productivity results when people simply do not work hard. In managing people, or in being managed, we must maximize our time. To "be all you can be" eventually results in a pay raise.

The Proof, Need I Say More?

I once had an administrative assistant who was wonderful. She was great with people, had a natural aptitude for watching the books, handled the telephone very well, and excelled in a myriad of secretarial skills. When I lost everything, I had to let her go; however, I had no trouble placing her in a better-paying job. Not only did she get a raise after leaving me, she has since moved up through that company like a rocket. Thus, she reached a much better position than the one I offered her. Everyone that had contact with my company had been impressed with her positive outlook and ability to get things done. She wasn't doing things for my company in order to get a better job later; she simply did what was asked and a little more, every time.

That is true of any position in any field. You must first be committed to working hard, and then the results will come.

Matthew 7:12 *"Therefore whatever you want men to do to you, do also to them . . ."*

Work Hard

During a period of economic hardship caused by high interest rates in the real estate business, my mother sent me the following poem, which still hangs on my office wall today. Her note read, "This was a Depression-era poem. Strange, it still applies today."

The Rooster & The Hen

Said the Little Red Rooster,
"Believe me, things are tough!
Seems the worms are getting scarcer
And I cannot find enough.
What's become of all those fat ones?
It's a mystery to me.
There were thousands through that rainy spell,
But now, where can they be?"

But the Old Black Hen who heard him
Didn't grumble or complain,
She had lived through lots of dry spells
She had lived through floods of rain.
She picked a new and undug spot;
The ground was hard and firm,
"I must go to the worms," she said.
"The worms won't come to me."

The Rooster vainly spent his day
Through habit, by the ways
Where fat round worms had passed in squads
Back in the rainy days.
When nightfall found him supperless,
He growled in accents rough,
"I'm hungry as a fowl can be;
Conditions sure are tough."

But the Old Black Hen hopped to her perch
and dropped her eyes to sleep
And murmured in a drowsy tone,
"Young man, hear this and weep.
I'm full of worms and happy
For I've eaten like a pig.
The worms were there as always
But, boy, I had to dig!"

Thoughts from Sharon . . .

After finishing college, marrying, and moving to Nashville, I needed a job. I looked and looked not knowing what I wanted to do. At that time I was not interested in the degree area I had chosen during college, although I now realize my degree did pay off.

I became a loan processor at a local financial institution. I loved this job. I worked with a group of great people and a great company.

After several years of marriage, Dave and I decided it was time to start a family. Now I had a big choice to make. Do I stay home with a new baby, or do I continue working? I made the best choice: I became a stay-at-home mom. I feel very blessed and privileged to have this type of career.

Choosing a career is an important step in everyone's life. What a big decision one person has to make! Ask yourself this important question: What do I want to do and what can I do best?

We all have different qualities and aptitudes. You know certain areas where you excel. You need to use the gifts you have.

Enjoy what you do and do your best. The rewards will always pay off.

Peace Puppies

1. **Avoid "Stuffitis"—**The Worship of "Stuff"
2. **Plant Seeds—**Give Money Away to Worthy Causes
3. Develop Your Own **"Power over Purchase"**
4. **Find Where You Are Naturally Gifted—**Enjoy Your Work and Work Hard

CHAPTER SEVEN

Lifestyles of the Rich

THE FIRST LESSON of this chapter is to avoid the lifestyles of the rich *when you are not rich.* I have learned that the best things in life, including good "stuff," come only at the expense of personal discipline. Many of my suggestions may not appear "fun" in the short run, but in actuality they are a lot more "fun" in the long run. Henry David Thoreau once observed, "Almost any man knows how to earn money, but not one in a million knows how to spend it."

No Way Around It

You must limit your style of living. You must figure out what your actual income is and then proceed to live far below that mark. You may respond, "That is impossible!" No, it is not impossible; difficult, maybe, but not impossible. It will take some time to undo some of the messes you have gotten yourself into and this book will help you—but it is very possible.

Experts have tracked the baby boomers' financial growth and spending habits for years. What they have found is that although most couples are broke when they get married, within three or four years they have attempted to copy their parents' net worth and lifestyles. Larry Burkett notes that with the broad spectrum of borrowing available, many young couples can quickly have almost the same lifestyle that it took their parents twenty-five years to achieve. These couples drive the same cars and live only blocks away—except they may have a newer house and nicer clothes than their parents, who make more money and have worked a lifetime to attain these possessions. The only problem is that the new couple has covered themselves with every imaginable type of debt, and their financial ship is very unsteady. Why? Because they could not say no to themselves.

Here's How It Starts

The normal scenario goes like this: Joe and Sue get married and have no assets. I mean, they are *b-r-o-k-e.* It is a time of "Honey, we don't need money; we got love," and it's a good thing too because they are eating off a card table and driving a fifteen-year-old Pinto. Joe and Sue—and many of us—started housekeeping this way, but then everything expanded quickly. That neat new job had a neat new paycheck that went with it, and Joe and Sue had to find something to do with all that money. So they began to buy "stuff" and finance most of the purchases. The new cars had notes, as did the stereo, the waterbed, and that new house; all had payments. Here is Joe and Sue's financial situation after three to five years of marriage.

Income (Monthly)		**3,500**
minus—		
House Payment	875	
Equity Line	120	
Car Payment*	310	
Miscellaneous	115	
Utilities	430	
Gas Card	85	
MasterCard	120	
Visa	95	
Food	600	
Car Repair	75	
Clothes	100	
Car Insurance	120	
Life Insurance	75	
Car Gasoline	180	
Net Disposable Income		**200**

*(old second car is paid for)

This is a typical budget for a middle-class couple, and if these numbers hit close to home, it is because I've seen thousands of these situations. Some items will vary from region to region, but we will use these numbers for our discussion.

So Joe and Sue have $3,500 coming in and $3,300 going out. This budget does not account for many other things—a disaster looking for a place to happen, as we well see later. Let's say that Joe makes $2,400 per month gross. One day he comes home all excited because he has gotten a 10 percent raise.

Do We Slow Down? Of Course Not!

Things have been awfully tight lately. However, there is the matter of that old car, Sue reminds him. It does seem to break down a lot. They decide they need to go car shopping, and they promptly fall in love with this wonderful, new, bright red car, and, after all, the dealer did give them a great trade-in on that old clunker. (I heard a man say once that the worst car accidents happen on the showroom floor.) So here is what they buy:

> $16,000 car financed over 7 years at 14 percent with payments of $300 per month. Value of car after 7 years is about $800.

So Joe and Sue got a take-home raise of $200 per month and then promptly committed to an additional payment of $300 per month. Unfortunately, this process is the normal one. They now have income of $3,700 and outflow of $3,600, and their tight situation is even tighter. If they were going to commit to spend $300 per month, however, they could have done this:

> $5,400 car financed over 7 years at 14 percent means payments of $100 per month. Value of car after 7 years is about $400. The other $200 per month saved at 10 percent for 7 years is going to grow to $24,190.
>
> Or they could have saved the new $200 per month for one year ($2,400) and paid cash for a newer used car after selling the second car.

Now, what do you think would have been the best choice?

Whoa, Boy!

You have to remember to slow down! You must evaluate carefully your purchase decisions because if you will sacrifice for a few years, you can live easier later. Instead, if you strap yourselves to all these lifestyle purchases to live well, you actually cause an ongoing cancer that will prevent you from ever living well.

While in pursuit of the elusive brass ring, people often get involved with get-rich-quick approaches to business. You have to be wary of these risky ventures. If you limit your lifestyle, you can avoid this pitfall because you will be focused on long-range security.

Within the first couple of years after college I invited several very wealthy people out for dinner in order to pick those successful brains. One gentleman in his seventies who had acquired much wealth over his lifetime as a shopping center developer was nice enough to allow this aggressive young man to buy his dinner.

After about an hour of my asking, digging, and probing him for answers as to how I might duplicate his success, he finally looked me square in the eye and said, "Boy, seems to me you want to know how to get rich quick." To which I replied, "Of course." He paused a long time to add suspense and then said, "The best way to get rich quick is to *not* get rich quick."

Now, years later, I have often thought of that man and his very wise advice, particularly when I sit and cry with some couple who have tried so hard to live like the wealthy when they weren't and who have set themselves up for financial disaster. In his book *Money Talks,* Bob Edwards says, "If one-half of a man's schemes turned out according to his preliminary figures, he would have nothing to do but spend his money." It doesn't work that way.

You Can Always Spend It

You must limit your style of living, because you can always spend more than you can make. I have counseled people who make $200,000 annually and people who make $20,000, and they both spent it all. Yes, the guy with $200,000 had bigger toys and more sophisticated bad investments, but they both had the same result—*b-r-o-k-e*.

Having been in business several years in Nashville, Tennessee (Music City, USA), I have had the pleasure of seeing some fortunes made in the music business. A personal friend was a writer for one of the very well known country music groups a few years back. One day he called, all excited, to say that two songs he had cowritten were on some group's latest album. I thought, So what? No big deal. Just half-writer royalties on two songs that don't go single is nothing huge.

The Big Time

This songwriter went from $700 per month to over $50,000 per month for the next four or five months. He proceeded to do what any red-blooded American would do. He began to buy "stuff," *lots of* "stuff." On Thursday he drove up in front of our home to show us his $40,000 black convertible sports car. Then his cowriter pulled in behind him. They had bought matching black convertibles and had paid full sticker price. On Saturday he drove up with a new dual-wheel truck loaded with options; attached to the back of it was a thirty-six-foot mini-yacht. He had bought the boat and didn't have a way to pull it, so he bought the truck. A few months later, of course, the checks stopped as the album peaked and died, but the payments he had obligated for didn't stop. Today he is bankrupt and writing songs for $700 per month again.

Not Me, Never Me

You say, "That will never happen to me," but I bet it already has, only in a smaller fashion. Remember what Joe and Sue did with their raise? The same thing my friend did. Both parties immediately raised their standard of living to keep up with the income increases. Instead, why not keep the same style of living? I know it is tempting to treat yourself—and I have done it myself—but I have learned that I sacrifice the future when I do.

Most of our society defines a financial genius as someone who can make money faster than he can spend it. We are beginning to learn differently. At age twenty-six I owned over $4 million worth of real estate, and I thought I was hot "stuff." I was so cool that I didn't want to be seen in possession of anything that wasn't considered expensive, so I threw away an old leather briefcase that was functional and purchased a very expensive leather case. Of course, the latches on this expensive case broke within six months. About that time I was beginning to understand some of these principles of money, so I made myself carry that "expensive" case with no latches under my arm for two years to remind myself that more expensive isn't always better.

What Does It Matter?

Often when I speak before a crowd, I show my watch, which has a brand name no one has ever heard before. I tell them this watch is the latest fad, the very best quality known to man to date, and all the millionaires want one, but they are hard to find. I will even take the watch off and let someone hold it while telling them it cost over $6,000. After everyone is sufficiently impressed, I will tell them the truth, which is that all those statements are lies. The watch was purchased at a discount department store for $19.95 on sale. I know you may think that you would never fall for that, but this particular watch is reasonably attractive, and most people believe me. I use this example to illustrate the ridiculous purchases we sometimes make. Whether that watch cost $6,000 or $20 is irrelevant to anyone but my family because it tells time and is acceptably attractive. It is only relevant to my family because of what it did to or for my household budget.

You see, we have gradually slipped. It's happened so gradually that many of us did what we would never intellectually admit to doing. . . . We let some yuppie client or neighbor influence what we thought was important. I can hear you now: "Please don't say it!" I have to. We started acting as if we really did need to keep up with the Joneses. "Oh, no, not me," you say. I challenge you to look at the major purchases you have made during the last three years and the motivations behind those purchases. That is the acid test.

This Is How the Really Rich Do It

Many wealthy people I meet really do live only upper-middle-class lifestyles. Many extremely wealthy people I know, those who have had wealth for many years, live lower-middle-class lifestyles and don't suffer in the least. They understand that a limited lifestyle is what got them there, and they forgot to increase their lifestyles even to what most people call tolerable conditions.

I once met with a man worth over $10 million. His office was furnished with black rotary phones, and in his "reception area," if you would call it that, there was a vinyl couch with cuts in the cushions from the springs coming through. I am not suggesting you dip to the poverty level, but it is interesting how some people who have wealth live.

Proverbs 21:20 *"In the house of the wise are stores of choice food and oil, but the foolish man devours all he has" (emphasis added).*

Thoughts from Sharon . . .

Spending money is always fun whether you have it or not. I can spend hundreds, thousands, and even millions in my mind in just a matter of minutes. It's fun to daydream of having the best of everything.

I would like to give some advice to every young person or young married couple: Don't waste money. I wish Dave and I had learned that valuable lesson years ago.

In order to become wealthy, here are some basic rules that I feel should be followed:

1. *Set up a budget.*
2. *Do not overspread.*
3. *Stick with the budget.*
4. *Buy the basics. You will be able to afford the best later.*
5. *Save, save, save.*

Peace Puppies

1. **Avoid "Stuffitis"—**The Worship of "Stuff"
2. **Plant Seeds—**Give Money Away to Worthy Causes
3. Develop Your Own **"Power over Purchase"**
4. **Find Where You Are Naturally Gifted—**Enjoy Your Work and Work Hard
5. **Live Substantially Below Your Income**
6. **Sacrifice Now** So You Can Have Peace Later
7. **You Can Always Spend More Than You Can Make**

CHAPTER EIGHT

Dumping Debt

THE TOUGHEST JOB of persuasion I have in this entire book comes in this chapter. If I have built some credibility with you to this point, I now stand a chance of losing it. If you believe something to be true—I mean really believe something to be true, so true you have bet on it—then if I challenge that view I stand a real chance of discrediting myself and whatever good I have done to this point. Your view or belief system is called your paradigm. Your paradigm is your filter system. If you receive information that does not match your belief system, you filter it out—and usually with it that kook that brought you that bad information.

Bad Road Maps

The scary thing about your paradigm is that it is based on your past and your feelings. What if it was wrong? What if your feelings and your past gave you a road map that sent you toward Maine when your goal was Florida? It could be a long trip. I was recently reading a book called *Partners with God* when I was reacquainted with a horrible story widely reported in the press.

A Really Bad Road Map

One of the worst experiences is watching a loved one die a slow, painful death. Thirty-five-year-old Linda Welch had the horrible job of nursing her mother through the pain, suffering, and finally death due to cancer. As the cancer destroyed her mother slowly, she had to sit and watch, doing nothing except to attempt whatever minor comforts she could provide. As the disease took its toll on her mother, Linda too was affected with her own fear and sorrow.

A severe and persistent sore throat several months later gives the story a macabre twist. Linda believed it was cancer. She knew she could not endure the same pain and suffering that she had just walked through with her mother. She felt the world was a cruel place and her children would be better off in heaven with her. The six notes the Jefferson County, Missouri, Sheriff's Department found indicate that the mother of two was deeply distraught about the cancer. And so Linda turned a gun on five-year-old Crystal, then shot Steven Jr., only ten, and finished the deed with suicide.

She acted on what she really believed to be true. If you

had asked her she could have given you a passionate and deeply held position about why this course of action was the *only* way. The horror is that an autopsy revealed that Linda had strep throat and the flu, not cancer at all.[1]

Go Play in the Traffic

Acting on incorrect information, no matter how deeply held, can be catastrophic; at the least it is painful. That stupid saying "What you don't know can't hurt you" is ridiculous. What you don't know can kill you. If you don't know that tractor trailer trucks hurt when hitting you, then you can play in the middle of the interstate with no fear—but that doesn't mean you won't get killed.

A Challenge

I challenge you in these next few pages to keep an open mind. Allow your paradigm, your belief system, to drop, and you just might learn something. Let's look at stretching or shifting your visual paradigm to show you how this works:

IAMNOWHERE

I AM NOWHERE

I AM NOW HERE

While you probably saw one version first, you will never see that again and miss both of the others.

I Hope There Is a Point to This

I am not suggesting that you are suicidal, but your road map to finances may be that far off. I am going to ask you to consider something that will seem ridiculous and un-American. Some of you have been in a "financial wreck" that ripped pain through your family and your soul, causing permanent scars. Some have even lost a spouse to divorce due to the financial stress. You will read what follows with an open mind. Some of you have never even had a small dent in your financial car door. So you will probably not even read this whole chapter, and you will likely view me as having little sense. What I have to report to you, from observing national trends and people in pain, is going to be hard to swallow. Nevertheless, I am duty bound to tell you: *Dump Debt.* That's right—do not borrow money.

You Communist!!

You may say, "What?! How un-American! Only Communists don't borrow money! How can a capital-driven society possibly survive if there is no debt?" Well, it can survive and you can survive, *yea,* even prosper! This problem of consumers, companies, and even nations loading themselves with debt is an aggressive, fast-spreading, and financially deadly cancer. I refer you to your own budget and to the statistics earlier in the book. We borrow as if we have forgotten that we have to pay it back. *We do!* Look at it from the positive side; if you had no debt, how much money could you save every month? How much could you give every month? How much would you have to earn if you had no payments? If you look at what we have learned about compound interest and bargain hunting, with a totally freed-up budget you could be wealthy, wildly wealthy, within just a few years. But we are strapped with debt.

Debt Is a Product

When you go into the furniture store to browse, and the salesperson comes to ask, "May I help you," you always say, "Oh, no, I'm just looking." Why? Because we all know that furniture stores are in it for the money. They have a product line like sofas, dining room suites, and bedroom suites, and if you buy one they make a profit, for shame! So we build up sales resistance and say, "I'm just looking." I have a secret for you: banks are not nonprofit companies. They have a product line too; they sell debt—MasterCard and Visa, Gold MasterCard and Visa, Platinum MasterCard and Visa, Plutonium MasterCard and Visa, home equity loans, home mortgages, car loans, car leases, student loans—and they all are for profit. Santa Claus did not build those tall bank buildings; you did. The only difference between the bank and the furniture store is that in the furniture store we say, "I'm just looking"—

but we crawl on our hands and knees into the bank lobby begging to buy their product: "Give me one of each, oh please."

And banks are aggressively marketing their products. MasterCard, Visa, American Express, and Discover will spend a combined $567 billion this year alone in advertising.[2] BAI Global says there were slightly more than 5 billion direct-mail solicitations sent out for credit in 2001. Seventy-nine percent of households (eight of ten homes on your street) received an average of five credit card offers per month the same year.[3] Citibank, the largest issuer of Visa, will spend $10 million this year just marketing credit cards to your high school and college student.[4] Isn't that exciting? To add insult to injury, the college can earn $50,000 to $100,000 per year just to allow a credit card company to operate on campus.[5] Credit cards have become a rite of passage.

Now that the baby busters and the younger boomers are growing older, the platinum and gold cards are losing their false appeal, so now the marketing is moving toward the "affinity" cards. Your teenager doesn't care about gold cards, but he would love the new Star Trek card, or he could be one of the first 15,000 to have signed up in the first month for the Rolling Stone card featuring Mick Jagger's lips and tongue.[6] And a Nashville bank has issued the new credit-on-country line of cards featuring Reba McEntire's face or Alan Jackson's mug on your plastic. The banker who designed that program had the audacity to state in the press release: "It's a win-win situation for the bank and the artist."[7] What about the consumer winning? Sounds like you weren't figured in their equation.

> **Proverbs 22:7** *The rich rule over the poor and the borrower is servant to the lender (emphasis added).*

We consumers have become a nation of servants to financial institutions. We used to joke that a bank was where you could borrow money if you could prove you didn't need it. Now, with the advent of aggressive credit marketing strategies, we can borrow even when we shouldn't be allowed to. We are sold credit in so many ways by so many people that we end up buying a *lot* of it, meaning we borrow money. We borrow money not just because it is made easy for us, but because we are sold on the convenience, perceived prosperity, and fun that all that "stuff" and associated debt are supposed to bring us. Let's look at some of these financial products and discover where we *really* are with them.

The Rest of the Story

I mean, we are getting in deep. *The Consumer Reports Money Book* states that the typical household debt totals more than $38,000.[8] In addition, *Consumer Reports* says we have over 1 billion pieces of plastic[9] with one of the major cards in 74 percent of all households.[10] You are weird if you don't have a credit card; that is definitely market saturation. Even in spite of this, some of you are sitting there shaking your head at this poor backwoods thinking author for suggesting something as radical as no debt. But of course *you* would never abuse borrowing—seems that I heard an alcoholic tell me that once about drinking.

Credit Cards

The easiest thing to convince you not to use is credit cards. The typical cardholder carries seven cards[11] that were accumulated by a design no more logical than just who sent him one. Many an expert has written on the evils of credit cards. They are dangerous and horrible financial tools. The convenience of plastic makes you buy "stuff" you would never buy otherwise. The advertisements purport that you will have more social status, glamour, and fun by using their super platinum gold titanium card. I remember years ago when I got my first American Express Gold Card, I really thought I was hot stuff. If your self-esteem is drawn from the "metal" of your plastic, you have missed the boat. Go home.

Having Fun Yet?

You get the *perceived plastic prosperity* disease when you appear prosperous, but are digging a grave. You see no cash pass from your hand, and so you register very little emotional realization that you've just spent money.

On average, cardholders carry a $8,367 balance on their cards from month to month (160 percent increase since the past decade), paying an average 18.3 percent in interest. That amounts to $929.70 a year in interest payments according to RAM Research Corp.[12] The CCCS online survey of 5,000 participants found that 80 percent of consumers state that their credit cards are at or near their maximum credit limit and that 37 percent have taken cash advances from one credit card to make monthly payments on another credit card as reported to CardWeb.[13] One hundred eighty-five million U.S. consumers have credit cards and 200 million new cards were issued in 2000 alone according to Card Track.[14]

Sears has 63 million cardholders, according to Sears Investor's financial report. Sears averages 12,054 credit card applications a day and 361,643 per month according to *The Pittsburgh Post-Gazette*. According to *The Wall Street Journal,* Sears charges a 21 percent annual rate and its finance income accounts for over 40 percent of operating income . . . analysts say Sears is as much a finance company as a retailer. Sears has signed up more than 20 million consumers for its Gold MasterCard, which was launched two years ago. Target is leading the way as the fastest growing VISA issuer while Sears is leading the MasterCard pack. Target has moved into the top 25 of U.S. card issuers as its VISA outstanding debts have topped $2 billion.[15]

American Express has 47.9 million cardholders according to Reuters with more than 60,000 employees. They can truly be called America Excess.[16] Many Americans, more than 50 million, have "Discover"ed bondage.

Are you having fun yet? Feeling like you have been sold, sold, sold by big, big business? Well we have all been sold—sold on making credit card companies rich.

But you say, "Dave, I pay mine off every month." Maybe, maybe not. BankCard Holders of America says that 70 percent of cardholders carry a balance with an average interest rate of 18.3 percent.[17] Even if you do pay it off, you buy more when using plastic. Kroger has issued its new co-branded MasterCard, not only because of the interest the company will make, but also because studies have shown that the typical grocery purchase almost doubles when the shopper uses plastic.[18] So it didn't cost you anything? This year Americans will put $10 billion of groceries[19] on credit cards. Talk about financing a depreciating asset—it's prime rib financed for thirty-nine years. Last warning: 72 percent of the cards have variable interest rates, which means your debt will go up if rates do. Interestingly, only 17 percent of cardholders realize that their rate is variable.[20] I think after looking at it from the bank's side I will start a DaveCard. Want one?

How many times have you gone out to eat or bought clothes or even taken a vacation that you could not afford, and you borrowed the money through plastic purchases at lousy rates and terms? I have done it, and so have most of you, but this is bad, bad planning and use of your funds. I have not had a credit card for years now. Many people tell me that they can control it. Therapists who specialize in addictions say that the first level of treatment always involves denial, which they consider to be a strong indicator that there is an addictive problem.

More Sad Stuff

I recently counseled a couple in their forties who had been married for over fifteen years. These were very upright, moral people who had a little trouble with their finances. He had been laid off, but they maintained their two-income lifestyle, accumulating $50,000 in credit card debt. When they could not pay the monthly bills, they came to us for help. In over fifteen years they had never been one day late on a payment to anyone, but now they were committed to $3,200 more per month than they had coming in.

They ended up losing everything they owned. They tried to start over, but the financial stress and the destruction of trust ended their marriage. In the last couple of years we have had normal, scared people in our offices with real credit card debt of $23,000, $44,000, $53,200, $63,400, $74,600, $84,000, and the record to date: $323,400 in credit card debt!!! I guess your $15,000 feels better now, but please don't tell me you can control your plastic, because I have seen too much pain that proves otherwise.

Debit Cards

If you are normal you are asking, "If I get rid of my plastic, how will I rent a car or hotel room, or purchase by phone?" The new Visa and MasterCard debit cards solve the problem. Anywhere Visa is accepted the Visa debit card is taken; as a matter of fact, I just give them my Visa number. The merchant treats it just like a Visa, but it comes out of your checking account that night, just like an ATM withdrawal. I have debit cards on my personal and business accounts for convenience, but I never use them except for travel because, remember, you spend less when using cash. If you save your first $1,000 toward your emergency fund and get a debit card, then there is no possible reason not to have . . .

Plastic Surgery

Stop reading right now and have a family meeting. Let each member participate in a candlelight ceremony at which each takes part in a plastic surgery party. That's right, cut them up.

Home Equity Loans

Home equity loans. Bankers call them HELs, but I think they just left off an "L." Current tax law makes it advantageous tax-wise to borrow on your home rather than on other goods. Have you forgotten that this is your home—you know, a basic need, like shelter? Many Americans currently have a roof over their family, but they will risk that just for the sake of sophistication, tax advantage, or, worse yet, a vacation like the ads describe. Home equity loans have had explosive growth as Americans try to borrow their way out of debt. The most predatory of these loans is the stupid practice of borrowing more on your home than it is worth. You can borrow 125 percent of your home's value—dumb, really dumb. You are then stuck and will be foreclosed if you don't make the payments. Financially it is like pouring gas over your head and handing the local finance company manager a lit match, then holding your breath.

Amazing what a tax law change followed by a little marketing will do to our sensibilities. As real estate has declined in value in many areas, we need to remember that we might have to end up writing a check in order to sell that home someday. Many noted publications have said home equity loans are the next big downfall of the consumer, and I am beginning to see too many in foreclosure. Beware!

Regular Mortgages

Regular home loans are probably the best buy you can get, in general. The interest rates and terms are about the best of any borrowing available to the consumer. The worst home loans are the adjustable rate mortgages, or ARMs. These mortgages normally adjust annually based on what another rate does. Most of these adjustments are based on indexes like the one-year treasury bills (T-bills) or on the 11th district cost of funds index for the Federal Home Loan Bank Board.

The T-bill is the more volatile of the two, but neither is acceptable in terms of risk. The *Wall Street Journal* has reported that many financial institutions "forget" to lower the rate (strange how they never "forget" to raise it). A fixed-rate shorter-term loan on a home is your best bet, and I will expand on that later.

By the way, if you have too many open credit card accounts, even with zero balances, the mortgage company will count it against you when qualifying for a mortgage.[21]

Auto Loans

Auto loans are terrible because, unless on a very short term (three years or less), the value of the car normally drops much faster than the loan balance, leaving you in a precarious position. Most auto loans go on far too long and charge a premium interest rate as opposed to the prime rate. The typical car loan today is $375 per month with fifty-five months to pay.[22] Plus, when you finance a car you cannot get as good a buy, so you are paying extra again.

The worst deal on the car lot today is the car lease. *Consumer Reports* says the most expensive way to purchase an auto is the lease.[23] Most auto leases by the major companies are currently figured on 15 percent yield based on what the car will be worth at the end of the lease. You are paying within a few dollars per month of a straight finance plan and do not own the car at the end of the term. Possibly the worst feature of most leases is that you are trapped for the period of the lease and most families trade cars more often than five or seven years. Yes, you can trade with that dealer and many times get out of the lease for a penalty, but again, you are paying a premium.

Why do dealers push leases and financing? The typical new-car sale nets the dealer only $82, but if you lease it the dealer's profit is between $1,000 and $1,300.[24]

You do not have to borrow money to buy a car. Pay cash for one that is not quite what you want, start saving the equivalent of a car payment a month, and very soon you can drive whatever you want. By sniffing out great deals and selling every so often, I drive almost free. I'll bet you agree "free" beats a lease.

Anatomy of a Repo

Let's look at what can happen to you if you have financial problems after financing a new car. If you buy a new $18,000 car and finance it for seven years at 13 percent, payments will be $327 per month. What happens if you get laid off after one year of ownership and cannot pay the payments? The car is now worth an average of $13,000, but you owe $16,800. You cannot sell it for what you owe, and the finance company repossesses it.

When they sell it on the repo lot it will bring about $9,000, leaving you still owing $7,800, for which they will chase you to the ends of the earth. You may be able to settle with them on this $7,800 deficit by making payments, if you are lucky. But it is very hard to make payments on a car you no longer own. I have met many people who have had to endure this scenario.

Foreclosure on a house creates a similar situation, except you can add a zero to the end of the figure causing the problem. Many bankruptcies are filed every year due to this leftover debt after repo.

Many say, "How could the bank possibly expect me to pay the difference?" Simple, because you signed a loan agreement obligating yourself personally. This is called personal liability, which means regardless of what happens to the item you pledged for the loan (the collateral) you still owe the money. If they don't get enough from the collateral you are legally obligated for the balance.

Should you total the car in a wreck and owe more than what the car is worth, in all likelihood you will get an insurance check for the value and you will still owe the difference. I have seen this problem more than once. Most people have no idea what those loan agreements that they are signing mean. Because you are personally liable, if you do not pay that balance (called a deficit), the lender will sue you for it, and they will win the suit.

Then It Really Gets Rough

Upon winning the suit, if you still cannot pay, they will execute on the suit. This means that they will begin to collect things of yours to sell, and the proceeds are applied to the balance. They will attach, and clean out, savings and checking accounts. They will garnishee your wages, which means the court orders your employer to pay the court the majority of your check until you have paid the balance. They can come to your home with a warrant and take your furniture, including your baby bed, and sell it to pay on your balance. You will truly begin to see that the *borrower is the servant to the lender.*

Should you happen to have an account with the bank that you defaulted on, the loan agreement you signed probably gives them the right to clean out that account even without a lawsuit and apply that money to your deficit balance. If you have other loans with the bank in default and pay off your car, they probably do not have to give you the title until all loans are paid in full, because of what is called a "dragnet clause" in the loan document.

Basically, if you do not pay on any loan, they will own you until you do. The only escape is payment or bankruptcy. The laws and mechanics for collection of defaulted loans in your state may differ slightly from those listed above, but they will collect somehow, unless you file bankruptcy. Benjamin Franklin said, "Creditors have better memories than debtors."

Finance Companies and Thrifts

Perhaps the most expensive money comes from consumer finance companies. These companies specialize in higher-risk loans and charge very high interest rates. If your state does not have a cap on interest rates you will usually find these companies charging up to 25 percent per year. These companies finance furniture, stereos, waterbeds, appliances, electronic equipment, and so on. If you remember the "let the buyer beware" chapter, these companies are the ones that buy the "ninety days same as cash" contracts, because you will seldom pay those off in ninety days. Over 70 percent of them convert to 24 percent loans with prepayment penalties.

Also, beware of low-rate bait credit cards. Many folks shift to lower-rate cards in an effort to win the debt game. Beware, most of these cards go up dramatically at the end of a year. If you are late more than three times on the new American Express True Grace Optima Card, your rate will go up to 20.65 percent—that is *true grace*.[25]

Debt Consolidation

These companies also do a lot of debt consolidation or bill consolidation loans. Let's look at a bill consolidation loan for the average couple. Joe and Sue have the following debt they wish to consolidate:

Item	Balance	Payment	Interest Rate
Visa	1,200	200	18
MasterCard	1,700	250	18
Doctor	400	100	18
Gas Card	600	80	18
Car	6,500	270	12
Furniture	3,500	175	15
TOTAL	13,900	1,075	

What Else Can I Do?

These bills are causing "great strain" for Joe and Sue. If only they could get some relief! So they go the friendly finance company that will lend them not only enough for the bills, but even a little extra so they will have some extra cash. But let's say they borrow just the $13,900 and they want to cut their payments in half so they'll have a payment of $550 per month. They will pay that for thirty-six months, for a total of $19,800.

This is an extremely poor program because if they could have just worked extra or figured out any way to hold out, in just nine months they could have paid off everything—using the snowball method—except the car and the furniture. The total payments would then be only $445 per month and the two outstanding items will be paid off in two years instead of three years, and at a lower interest rate. Beware of bill consolidation. Few cases justify using this strategy.

The Friendly Loan

Have you ever loaned money to or borrowed money from a friend or relative? This is the best way I know to lose a friendship or strain a relationship. The borrower feels awkward even being in the same room with the lender, and if something goes wrong, most friendships are destroyed. That is because we have become the servant or the master, not just "Joe" anymore.

Co-Signing Is Not Very Bright

If you are going to avoid borrowing money, you should definitely avoid co-signing for someone else's loan. When you co-sign, you borrow the money. The professional money lender who is trained when to, and when not to, loan money has decided this person should not borrow right now. However, we in our infinite wisdom know better so we sign for him. After all, we were just trying to help a friend or relative. Then when the loan goes bad the bank comes straight to us, because they know he doesn't have the money. I have co-signed for loans and been co-signed for and almost without fail it got me into trouble both ways. I have learned the hard way, and I am here to warn you about the pitfalls of co-signing notes.

For the Sophisticate

Now that we have reviewed the major areas and ways to borrow money, let's address one more issue for the finance major who has more sophisticated viewpoints or arguments. Without going into a lengthy and detailed explanation, I have run computer models on debt-free investment analysis. The concept of leverage is always brought up when I talk about being debt free. I have a thorough understanding of internal rates of return, net present value, simple return on investment, and a myriad of other measurements that we are taught show the power of using borrowed money on investments. The interesting thing is that seldom is a risk factor brought into the formula, thereby effectively reducing the perceived yield.

Sophisticates want to cross swords on this issue, but I think they will find that a reasonable risk factor (that risk is not present when debt free) reduces the advantages of leverage to zero in a closer look. Also, if you have done much business with European or Middle Eastern companies you have found that they exist on virtually no debt and do just fine. In our arrogance we think the "big crash" will never happen to us. Wrong.

I counseled a very sophisticated investor recently who once had a large net worth. He had borrowed $70,000 from a local bank to purchase two limited partnership shares in a real estate deal. The real estate company he purchased them through was nationally known and the largest in the Southeast. That company had been open for many years with a wonderful track record. They almost never lost money. In fact, they almost always exceeded the projected returns.

The horribly negative impact that the 1986 tax act had on the real estate world broke that company. That left the partners trying to run a large apartment complex in a metropolitan city five hundred miles away. They had leveraged into the deal (borrowed all they could) so there was very little equity, and with the downfall of income-producing real estate prices, the apartment complex actually became worth less than the mortgages. With negative equity the two limited partnership shares he had purchased to save on taxes and make money with were now worthless, but he still owed money on them. So he now owes the bank a $70,000 unsecured loan. He is having trouble paying that loan and will likely go into default. But he could "control" it, or so he thought.

You Really Come Out Much Better

Author Robert Ringer tells the story of a recently deceased friend of his who had the same horrible experience in the Great Depression of the 1930s that many people are having today. His personal home was foreclosed on and he had to start completely over. Because of the pain, this man vowed to *never* borrow money again from anyone. Over his lifetime he built a substantial fortune, and as his cash position grew his fortune grew faster and faster. His wealth grew at explosive rates because he never had losses due to payments, and because during down times he always had cash to make the great buys from distressed sellers. He bought office buildings, office equipment, cars, homes, and even entire companies for *cash,* always getting substantial discounts. At his death he was worth in excess of $500 million. Don't tell me it doesn't work!

If You Must

After all that, if you must borrow money, let me give you two basic guidelines. First, borrow on short terms and only borrow on items that go up in value. That means never on anything except possibly a home, which you should pay off as soon as possible. Next, the terms are very important. If you can, buy less, so that you can pay off faster, and then make sure you get a very low interest rate. For example, if you were to finance $80,000 on a home at 10 percent, here are two ways:

30 years	360 pymts. at $702/mo.	$252,720 total
15 years	180 pymts. at $860/mo.	$154,800 total
Total difference		$158 more, but **$97,920 saved**

Be careful, because well-meaning, well-trained real estate brokers will sell you all you can possibly afford on a thirty-year mortgage. They get paid on a percentage of the sales price, not on how much you save over fifteen years. Be sure you remember how much you save if you go with shorter terms.

If you already have your thirty-year mortgage in place, you can pay one or two extra payments per year to be applied to principal. For example, a $100,000, thirty-year mortgage at 10 percent will pay off in 21.1 years just by paying one extra payment per year.

OK, I Give. Now What?

You say, "Okay, okay, you win. I want out of debt and I want to stay out, but how do I do that?" There are two things you can do. The first method took years of research and many hours of development to get the concept in place. This highly sophisticated concept is top secret and is usually reserved for very special situations only. This first method to get out of debt is this:

In order to get out of debt:
quit borrowing more money.

Our problem is not getting out of debt; it is keeping out of debt. You can't get out of a hole by digging out the bottom. Almost all consumer loans are set up to pay off naturally, and just by paying the payments you will soon be completely debt free. Get *mad!!!* There is no energy in logic, only emotion. When you get ticked off you can get out. Years of counseling have revealed that this plan works. You can't scheme, scam, or borrow your way out of debt. You just have to get mad.

The Debt Snowball

The second way out involves accelerating the process. I first learned this technique through Larry Burkett's Christian Financial Concepts, but it is taught by many counselors concerned with debt reduction. We call this the "debt snowball." For example, let's look at another possible list of debts for Joe and Sue.

Item	Balance	Payment	Interest Rate
Visa	1,200	200	18%
Student Loan	7,000	123	9%
Car	6,500	250	12%
MasterCard	700	70	18%
Gas Card	400	60	18%
House	60,000	540	9%

The first step in this strategy is to put the debts in ascending order with the smallest remaining balance first and the largest last. Do this regardless of interest rate or payment. You will pay these off in this new order. I have read and found in actual experience that this works because you get to see some success quickly and are not trying to pay off the largest balance just because it has a high rate of interest. So our new order of attack will look like this:

Item	Balance	Payment	Interest Rate
Gas Card	400	60	18%
MasterCard	700	70	18%
Visa	1,200	200	18%
Car	6,500	250	12%
Student Loan	7,000	123	9%
House	60,000	540	9%

Pretend you're Joe, and I'll show you how this strategy works. Now Joe decides to work some overtime or Sue has a garage sale and you pay off the gas card in the first month. Next, *do not* spend the $60 per month you used to spend on the gas card; instead add $60 to the next payment on the list. You are then paying MasterCard $130 per month until paid. That will pay off in the seventh month. Then you add $130 to the $200 Visa payment so that you are paying $330. Because you have already been paying on Visa for seven months, it will pay off in the eighth month (the next month). So you add $330 to your car payment of $250, making your car payment $580. That will cause the car to be paid off in seventeen more months, only twenty-five months into our program. The happy ending of your story is that everything in our example (and yours will vary) is paid off in thirty-two months except the house.

Big Fun

Now you have $1,243 per month to pay on the house, and it will be paid for in five more years. As an alternative you could save $275 per month of the $1,243 to purchase a car with cash. When you pay the remaining $968, the house will pay off in just seven years, while the $275 per month saved will grow to $11,490 in just three years at 10 percent for your cash car purchase.

As these bills are paid off you will feel a peace and a change in your attitude about financial matters. You will begin to realize that they do not "matter" so much. I can speak from experience, as I have worked through a very large "debt snowball."

Now You Must Decide

Well, by this point you are either seriously considering what I have outlined in this chapter, or you think I am crazy. Are you the opposite of Linda Welch? Do you think you have a sore throat and in reality you have cancer of the wallet? I challenge you, you have tried it *their* way and it doesn't work, except for them. Try this new approach, you may find some very new consequences in your life. I know that suggesting you stay out of debt is radical and may seem utterly ridiculous, but I am tired of seeing grown adults on the brink of suicide, widows left with a legacy of debt, children who are taught by example that if I want it I get it *now*. Dump debt. If you don't, remember you are instantly the servant to the lender.

Proverbs 22:7 *The rich rule over the poor and the borrower is servant to the lender (emphasis added).*

Thoughts from Sharon . . .

Debt will always get you in trouble. Have you ever lain awake at night wondering which bills were going to get paid? Have you ever prayed the phone wouldn't ring when your best friend came over because it might be a collection agency? Have you ever wished you could buy something for your children but didn't have the money? Many of us have fought these problems over and over. How sad it is to live each day like this.

You need to get mad. First, you need to realize that you can stop borrowing. You can get out of debt. You can have a happy and better life. It takes a lot of willpower, but it can be done.

The debt snowball was a great method Dave and I used. First, we learned we had to stop borrowing. Second, we applied every extra penny we had that month to a certain bill. Yes, it was hard, but what a reward it was to watch debt after debt disappear.

We started to feel in control. I encourage you to try this method. When this step has been accomplished, you will begin to experience financial peace.

Peace Puppies

1. **Avoid "Stuffitis"**—The Worship of "Stuff"
2. **Plant Seeds—**Give Money Away to Worthy Causes
3. Develop Your Own **"Power over Purchase"**
4. **Find Where You Are Naturally Gifted—**Enjoy Your Work and Work Hard
5. **Live Substantially Below Your Income**
6. **Sacrifice Now** So You Can Have Peace Later
7. **You Can Always Spend More Than You Can Make**
8. **The Borrower Is the Servant to the Lender;** So Beware!

CHAPTER NINE

Cucumbers, Collectors, and Credit Reports

WHAT IS ONE of the dumbest plants you can think of? My vote goes to the cucumber—round, green, and good for very little except to make the perfect pickle if picked before maturity. The other two subjects we are to discuss in this chapter are also to be picked before maturity. If you let them lie on the vine, without stunting their growth, you will wish you hadn't. Cucumbers if let go can at least be used on a salad, but if you let a credit report problem or collectors go, they will spoil your whole dinner with indigestion.

I Want That Cleansing Feeling

How long has it been since you ordered your credit bureau report? A good rule of thumb is to check your report at least once every two years. Consumers and congressmen were recently outraged at the report by the U.S. Public Interest Research Group revealing that 70 percent of credit reports contain errors.[1] That other Joe Smith who didn't pay his bills on time was accidentally keyed into the computer on your file and you didn't even know it. The other possibility is that you have actually had some bad credit and that is why you are reading a book entitled *Financial Peace*. So you want to clean it up.

How to Mess It Up

We need to understand why a credit report is important and that will tell us what we cannot do. Remember in chapter 8, "Dumping Debt," we decided borrowing money was not the way to go, so you may be wondering why you need a clean credit record. First, many potential employers will pull a credit report as an indication of character so a job hunt could be harmed by an unclean report. Second, even when you do not borrow for cars, credit cards, or any consumer goods, many will go for a five- or ten-year mortgage to get your home and get debt free quickly. So many people who have a goal of being debt free want a clean report for a short-term mortgage.

Under no circumstances do you get one of those high-fee rip-off secured credit cards to "build your credit." All this does is confirm for the mortgage company that you have not learned your lesson. As a matter of fact, if you have several open credit card accounts with zero balances, most mortgage lenders will count that against you because the day after closing you could furnish your home at 18 percent interest. In the real world, you become bankable if you make all bad accounts right and then pay on time any open accounts, including rent for one to two years. If you have bad credit or you are just starting out, do not borrow to create a good credit report. You simply pay what you owe on time, even if it is only rent. A clean period of time, with all bad debt made good, a decent down payment, and a steady job record is enough to get you approved for most mortgages. Please do not borrow to build or clean credit.

We strongly recommend that you fix all credit report problems yourself. Do not hire one of these credit cleanup firms because you don't need it. There are some legitimate cleanup firms, but that industry abounds with scam artists, which is another reason to do it yourself. Please do not believe anyone who tells you that they can legally remove accurate information from your report. If you did what the report says, you'll have to live with it for a while, and if you don't believe me, you are setting yourself up for a disappointment and a con.

The Washing Machine

The Federal Fair Credit Reporting Act was passed in 1977 by Congress to dictate how the credit bureaus interact with the consumer. All information, good or bad, is removed seven years from date of last activity, except a Chapter 7 bankruptcy, which stays on a report for ten years. This act also deals with how to have an inaccurate entry corrected or removed from your report. There is *no* provision in the act, regulation, or rule that enables anyone to remove accurate information from a report and anyone who tells you otherwise is someone you should walk away from, or rather run away from.

If you have inaccurate information on your report, the act states that upon notification the bureau must correct the entry or remove the entire entry within a "reasonable time." Court cases since the act's passage have ruled "reasonable time" to be thirty days. To clean your report of inaccurate information you should write a letter to the bureau with a copy of your report attached, stating that you challenge the accuracy of that account entry. State in your letter: "Under the provision set forth in the 1977 Federal Fair Credit Reporting Act, I hereby request that your agency prove to me in writing the accuracy of the reporting of this account. Under the terms of the Act and succeeding court cases, you have 30 days to prove such accuracy or remove the account entirely from my report and I ask that you do so." You should send a separate letter for each inaccurate entry (use Letter #1 in the appendix) and you *ALWAYS* send them by certified mail, return receipt requested. The receipt comes back to you in the mail to tell you when the thirty-day fuse began to burn. You will have to follow up after the thirty-day mark because most of the bureaus are backed up and slow. You will find that they are seldom able to verify the correct information and so be firm in your request to have the entire entry removed. You will have to be assertive. Napoleon said, "Victory belongs to the most persevering."

The Federal Trade Commission is the agency that governs bureaus' activities, so that is where you should complain if you can't get a reasonable response. You should also check your state's Consumer Affairs Department. Three national bureaus handle credit reporting. You must check all three, and your local agency, which will also be an agent for one of the big three. The three national bureaus are TRW, TransUnion, and Equifax (see appendix).

Good People Sometimes Have Trouble

You may be reading this book to attempt to get in control. Collectors may be hounding you and your spouse to distraction. Well, I've been there, done that, and got the T-shirt. Some people who don't pay their bills are the true deadbeats and deserve the pain, but most people are honorable and will do most anything to get their life back once they get behind on debt payments. Those of you who are holding your nose in the air, beware, your upper lip will get sunburned or you may trip and find yourself right down with the rest of us. The trick for those of us who have seen the bottom is to not stay there.

When we get behind we meet these enchanting souls called collectors, who it seems live to make us miserable. As if we didn't know we were behind, as if we didn't have enough stress, these folks show up to be ignorant and in our face. I know they wouldn't be calling if the bill had been paid, but let us assume for a minute that for that month we had to choose between a credit card payment and food, what would you choose? I once actually counseled a young single girl in her twenties who had not eaten in two days because she made sure her plastic was paid on time to protect her precious perfect credit bureau report. We did feed her, but that shows you how out of balance this game of being behind can become.

All You Can Do Is All You Can Do

Logical, honorable people who are down in income will and should pay necessities first, followed by unsecured debt. Collectors know that logical people will pay the house payment first, so they have developed a collections science to reprioritize your life. They have discovered that the only way people will pay an unsecured creditor first is if they are not being logical—so the collectors are taught in "Collections 101" to "evoke strong emotion." By being emotional you will pay them *before* the utilities or house payment. So they will try for emotions like anger, fear, hate, and even friendship.

When we were going through our garbage, American Express called and asked my wife why she would stay with a man who wouldn't pay his bills. Needless to say, when Sharon called my office crying, I was livid—so livid I wrote them a check. Guess I showed them, or did I? Later they called back after Sharon and I learned that this was all a technique. This time she told the guy not to get his panties in a wad when he tried the exact same line.

The approach that works is stored in the computer and will be tried again and again until you no longer respond. A client of ours not long ago received a call from another major credit card company. Since she was in the shower, her nine-year-old answered. This collector convinced the nine-year-old that the sheriff was going to take her toys because Mommy didn't pay the bills. Many of you naive souls think I am exaggerating, but there are many more hair-curling true stories to go with these. If the stories weren't true, do you think I'd risk it in print?

Stop the Garbage

In 1977 another act was passed to deal with this kind of garbage. The Federal Fair Debt Collection Practices Act deals with how third-party collectors must behave. A third-party collector is normally a bill collector who does not work for the company you owe. However, court cases since the act was passed indicate that all collection efforts will be judged by these standards. No harassing calls can be made; and all calls should be between 8 A.M. and 9 P.M. (The reason we didn't file suit in the above cases is that the conversations were not taped, so we couldn't prove in court that these absurdities really occurred.)

Repeated calling and name calling are prohibited. If a collector is harassing you, just put him on notice that you are taping the calls to ensure that he is within the realm of the Federal Fair Debt Collection Practices Act and you will see a major change in attitude. Recording can be done easily by using the memo button on your answering machine, which is required equipment to make it through hard times.

If you are getting unwanted calls at your workplace, send a certified letter (return receipt requested to prove receipt) to the collector in question requesting that they no longer call you at your workplace, and they must stop, according to this act (see Letter #2 in the appendix). The act even allows you to send a cease-and-desist letter requesting that they no longer contact you in any way except to inform you of legal proceedings (see Letter #3 in the appendix). I do not recommend this move except in very extreme circumstances, such as if you can no longer work it out. You will want to settle the debt as soon as you are able.

No collector may garnishee wages or attach bank accounts without first suing in court and winning. The only exception to this is a law (which I believe is unconstitutional) that Congress passed allowing student loans in default to be garnisheed at the whim of the collector without due process. Ninety-five percent of the unreasonable conversations you will have with bill collectors are bluff and based in ignorance. Most collections operations in credit card companies are merely telemarketing pools. The collector has on a headset, is in a cubicle, is looking at a computer screen, and is a low-paid position. The average time on the job for collector pools is about ninety days, and most of these people couldn't get a job at your local convenience store.

I See a Light

It is time for you to see a light at the end of the tunnel, one that is not an oncoming train. The best way and the most honorable way out of debt is with a plan. You set your plan and your priorities, not your creditors; otherwise, they will drown you. The best way for them to get paid is for you to take control of your financial destiny. You and your spouse set your goals, work hard, work often, live on little, and get out so you never have to talk to people whose sole job is to technique you again. Don't get me wrong: people should pay their debts and there are legitimate collections firms who use reasonable procedures to collect unpaid accounts, but it is the abuses we see daily in our office that we want to help you walk through. Remember, hope cannot be taken from you; you must surrender it.

Thoughts from Sharon . . .

Collectors scared me to death several years ago. So many times, I remember the phone ringing and feeling really nervous about who the caller would be on the other end. (For some reason, this seemed to happen a lot when I had company. How embarrassing.)

I wondered, do I answer the phone or not? Sometimes I

didn't want to because I knew what question the caller was going to ask. "When will you be mailing your next payment?" "How much money will you be mailing?" "We need the account current." On and on, question after question.

Knowing we didn't have any money, I would promise the collector the account would be paid, no matter what.

Time after time, day after day this happened. What a sick feeling.

Eventually I learned a valuable lesson. This happens to everyone, not just me. I realized this "collector" was just a person like me. This was his job. Just a simple job. What could he do?

Our credit was already bad, so I realized what if we were late again. I knew the accounts that we owed would be paid. It was just a matter of time. We stood by our word that each bill would be paid in full. However, paying them would be done according to our time schedule.

Peace Puppies

1. **Avoid "Stuffitis"—**The Worship of "Stuff"
2. **Plant Seeds—**Give Money Away to Worthy Causes
3. Develop Your Own **"Power over Purchase"**
4. **Find Where You Are Naturally Gifted—**Enjoy Your Work and Work Hard
5. **Live Substantially Below Your Income**
6. **Sacrifice Now** So You Can Have Peace Later
7. **You Can Always Spend More Than You Can Make**
8. **The Borrower Is the Servant to the Lender;** So Beware!
9. **Check Your Credit Report** at Least Once Every Two Years
10. **Handle Credit Report Corrections Yourself**
11. Realize That the Best Way for Delinquent Debt to Be Paid Is for You, Not Collectors, to **Control Your Financial Destiny**

CHAPTER TEN

Pile Up Plunder

PILE UP PLUNDER. Save money. *Save money.* S-a-v-e m-o-n-e-y. You must save money. I do not know how to say it any more plainly. You must save some of what you make out of every check, or you will never acquire any peace in your finances. This is a very elementary principle, but *no one does it*. Many financial geniuses will read this book with their noses in the air and say, "This writer is really basic" or "Can't he be any more original than that?" but even they don't save money. We live in one of the richest countries in the world, and yet the average family does not have over $1,000 in the bank. The awful truth is that the U.S. Department of Commerce reports that the typical American saves 2.2 percent of after-tax income, while NLI Research says the average Japanese saved 27.9 percent of after-tax income. That is just not good enough, America![1]

Only You Can Prevent Forest Fires

Tax incentives can't help you save. Spouses who badger can't help. Employer savings programs can help, but only you and a change in your discipline can cause savings to occur. This chapter will give you reasons to save, but until you resolve to save—and are willing to give up something now so that you might have more peace later—savings will not occur.

A recent *Worth* magazine Roper poll revealed that 74 percent of those surveyed wanted money just to increase security[2]—and yet I just told you that we are saving only 4.7 percent, which is some security. Another poll published in *USA Today* stated that only 18 percent of baby boomers believe they will receive Social Insecurity—I mean Security—and yet they are saving only 4.7 percent of their income.[3] You would think they would be scared into saving if they don't believe Social Security will be there. Even if Social Security is there, it is not enough. At the current rate of wealth creation in America, by the year 2005, out of one hundred workers age sixty-five: one will be wealthy ($5 million net worth or more), four will be financially independent ($1 million–$4.9 million net worth), forty-one will *have* to continue working, and fifty-four will be dead broke according to The Bull & Bear Financial Report.[4]

I feel that you should have a goal of saving 10 percent of your take-home pay. You work and slave at your job to bring home the bacon. Then what happens? Your checkbook simply serves as a clearing account for the people you owe and the "stuff" you buy. The money goes in and *all* the money goes out instantly. Only the names are changed to protect the innocent. I know, because I did it that way for years too. If you work that hard, and most of you do, then it is time to put a new name on your list of bills.

Pay Me; Please Pay Me!

At the top of your list every week, write the amount of money you will give away—your charitable gifts. The very next line should be marked "Pay Me," and then list your bills and make sure they are paid. It is ridiculous for you to spend your entire life at your given occupation only to end up broke and discouraged because you did not write "Pay Me" at the top of the page.

Most people need something to help them have the discipline to save. There are many programs, called "forced saving plans," that can help. If you have access to a credit union, you can set up a payroll deduction savings plan. A portion of your paycheck is deducted and deposited before you get your check; that way, you don't have a chance to do anything else with it. Most local banks also have forced savings programs to help you force yourself to save. If you need to start this way, *do it*.

PAC Man

Many insurance companies and security brokerage firms use a PAC (Pre-Authorized Checking) withdrawal system. On a certain day each month a stated amount is automatically withdrawn from your checking account and deposited into the savings program of your choice. These savings programs are annuities, money markets, mutual funds, etc., which can be very good. However, you must take the time to understand what you are putting your money into or you can get stung by some of these programs. I do not recommend a life insurance policy as a place to build up your savings or cash value. You must be wary of these policies, which will be discussed in a later chapter.

The most effective way to save is by applying discipline over a period of time, as opposed to trying to save in big splashes. There are at least three main reasons to save money. First, you should save until you have built an emergency fund. Second, you should save for purchases to avoid debt. Third, you should save for wealth building.

Emergency Fund

If you are a big-income earner of $150,000 plus per year, you may have gone to a big time "financial planner" and paid him a fee of $2,000 or more per year to "advise" you on your financial plans. Most people do not make that kind of income, but we should learn from what these big-income earners are taught.

A good financial planner will tell you that first you should have three to six months of expenses in liquid savings just for emergencies. Liquid means your money is stored where you can get it very quickly and easily. An example is a simple bank savings account or a money market fund that has check writing capability. A certificate of deposit (CD) that has a large interest penalty for early withdrawal is not very liquid nor is an investment in rental real estate.

If you spend $36,000 a year, you should have $9,000 to $18,000 where you can easily get it before you do any other investing. I know that seems like a lot of money, especially when most have only $1,000 in the bank now, but here is why the experts tell us we should save so much.

Singing in the Rain

Do you remember your grandmother telling you to save for a "rainy day"? She was right. It will rain, so why not be in a position to cover the problem and be caught "singing in the rain" rather than crying? *Money* magazine states that 75 percent of families will have a major negative financial event in any ten-year period.[5]

Never has a couple come to me for crisis financial counseling who had an emergency fund of three to six months expenses. Remember Joe and Sue? After they bought that second car for $300 per month, their budget had $3,700 income and $3,600 outflow. I said that was a disaster looking for a place to happen because people are normally cruising along at a "tight" level when the devastating "unexpected event" occurs. Sue gets pregnant or Joe gets laid off or Joe gets hurt on the job or there is a death in the family and they must share the expense or one of the wonderful cars has a major breakdown or a child has an accident requiring major medical treatment or or or . . .

Of Boats and Torpedoes

Let's look at our friends Joe and Sue once again. Joe and Sue's financial boat is cruising along already loaded to the brim when they get a $3,000 to $10,000 torpedo in the form of an "unexpected event." Then they start sinking fast and they have to play "juggle the bills." You know the game—you decide who *doesn't* get paid this month. There's just too much month left at the end of the money. By the time they get to my office they have so many balls—er, I mean, bills—in the air that they are out of control. If they only had an emergency fund to cushion the blow from the "unexpected event" torpedo!

A Simple Test

Put this book down now. Hold your right hand up in front of you with your elbow bent. Now reach your left hand across the back of your wrist to where your finger tips touch your main artery and then check for pulse. Is your heart beating? If you are alive and walking around, things *will* happen to you that you don't think will. The only way you can avoid unexpected financial events is not to be alive—so they are *not* "unexpected" events, are they?

The basic truth is that you must plan for the unexpected, because it will happen. Although we don't know what form it will take, it will come. Cars do break; women do get pregnant; people do get hurt or die; businesses do lay people off. To think otherwise is naive. So you have to plan for it. One of my friends said her grandmother taught her to have a G.O.K. fund—God Only Knows. Saving into an emergency fund first is an essential element for financial peace.

Saving for Wealth

Remember the "Money Is Active" principle. Here is where you can see just how active. Most consumers do not understand how quickly time, interest rates, and payments work for them or against them. At work on your money is a mathematical monster called compound interest. Compound interest can either be your best friend financially, if you make it work for you, or your worst possible enemy, if it works against you. If you are saving at good interest rates, every month, and for many years, compound interest is your best friend. However, if you have borrowed over long periods of time at high interest rates, you see it as your worst enemy.

Mathematically speaking, compound interest works exponentially or in a geometric progression. In English, this simply means that your money is affected by mathematical multiplied explosion, not by simple addition, such as $1+1=2$.

If you will look at the payment schedule on your house

of your car, you will see how the first bunch of payments are almost all interest and how you have paid back almost no debt. That is compound interest working against you. But it can also work just as strongly for you.

Watch Closely Now

Let me show you what I mean. If you start to save at age twenty-five with the idea that you will withdraw your money at age sixty-five, you will save for forty years. Let's say that you put $1,000 in a savings account one time at age twenty-five and you never deposited or withdrew anything from that account (you just let the interest compound or grow) until age sixty-five.

The Real Numbers

At 6 percent per year you would have just over $10,000 at age sixty-five, so if we double the interest rate to 12 percent you should have around $16,000, right? *Wrong!* You will have just over $93,000 at 12 percent at age sixty-five. That is compound interest working for you; you see the multiplication effect rather than the addition effect that most may have thought. But let's raise the rate of interest again—to 18 percent—and what will we have? $750,378!

Here's the Comparison:

- $1,000 one-time investment
- No withdrawal
- Age 25 to age 65 (40 years)

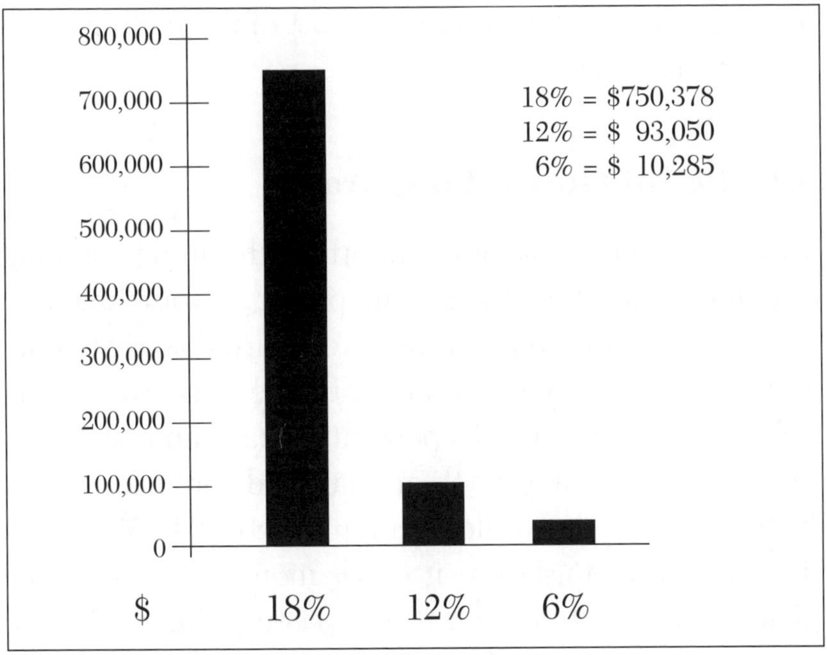

Can you see that the rate and term at which you save or borrow is very important? Now let me show you how banks make a profit. Do you have a bank credit card? Do you also have a savings account with that bank? Many people loan the bank their money in a savings account at 6 percent or less and then borrow their own money back by having a credit card balance and paying 18 percent. If you left $1,000 in a savings account like this and kept a $1,000 balance on your credit card, the bank will have made the spread at virtually no risk and with no investment for a $740,093 profit for every time this happens in our forty-year example. If you multiply this scenario times thousands of customers it is enough to make you understand how the banks own most of the tall buildings in every major city.

A Little Bit Goes a Long Way

To further show you how important the understanding of compound interest is and its power in your finances, let's look at retirement. Suppose you started at age twenty and saved for forty-five years until age sixty-five, saving only $65 per month at 12 percent average annual return (which a long-term growth mutual fund could easily do). In forty years you would accumulate $1,394,555 for retirement. You must save it *every* month. Saving is like planting an oak tree. You cannot keep pulling it by the roots to check its progress. There is no excuse why anyone, if he acquires the knowledge early enough, should not retire a millionaire. Compound interest is powerful, and remember, it works for or against you, with equal power.

Wow, What a Car!

Remember Joe and Sue? Let's look at them again. Remember they bought a $16,000 car for $300 per month. I said they should have waited and bought a $5,400 car for $100 per month and saved $200 per month at 10 percent for seven years, giving them $24,190 at the end. As long as they stay on the plan, they will have car payments for the rest of their lives, with compound interest working against them. However, using my second plan, we can imagine the scenario years into the future. By year seven the car is junk, in either plan, but suppose they saved that $24,190. Then they bought a $16,000 car for cash from that savings, leaving them $8,190.

The New Car

They now have a new car with no car payment and $8,190 in the bank, but let's go yet another seven years. They have no car payment, so instead of the $100 payment and the $200 savings they were doing each month, now they decide just to save $100 per month, freeing up $200 per month. At the end of seven more years, that $8,190 left over plus $100 per month plus 10 percent interest will now grow to $28,539. Now they again have a seven-year-old car that is worthless, so they buy yet another $16,000 car for cash, leaving $12,539 in savings. For another seven years they have no car payment and, though they do no additional saving, the $12,539 at 10 percent will grow to $24,436!

Pay Me Now or Pay Me Big Later

That is a hard chain of events to follow. The bottom line is that if Joe and Sue would sacrifice with a lesser purchase up front and save the difference, and then continue the process, they will be driving paid-for cars and have savings the rest of their lives. That is compound interest working for you. Again, the best way to get rich quick is *not* to get rich quick, but to watch your decisions and let time make you wealthy.

This idea—saving a certain monthly amount with interest in order to have the amount needed to make your purchases—is called "a sinking fund." The concept of a sinking fund is simple. It is making payments in reverse. If you want $4,000 for a dining room suite, why don't you use a sinking fund savings program instead of borrowing it at 24 percent? You can save $151 per month for 24 months at 10 percent—and then pay cash. (Note: 151 times 24 is only $3,624. The rest is interest in your favor.) But if you financed it at 24 percent at the furniture store, you would have paid $151 for 31 months, for a total of $4,681 for the same suite, not to mention the discount you should get for flashing cash (to be covered later).

All you need to design a sinking fund for any purchase is a simple financial calculator, or your banker can probably help you figure out your program, especially if you are saving in his bank. You need to always remember to make the power of compound interest work *for* you.

Who Is the Smarter—Ben or Arthur?

Bernard Zick, who has a master's degree in business administration (MBA) and is an expert in the time value of money, gave this consumer quiz in his monthly newsletter:

Ben, age nineteen, invests $2,000 per year compounded annually at 12 percent for eight years until he is thirty years old. For the next forty-six years, until he is sixty-five, Ben invests not one penny more.

Arthur, age twenty-seven, invests $2,000 per year for thirty-two years until he is sixty-five years old. His investment also earns 12 percent compound interest per year. At age sixty-five, will Arthur or Ben have the most money?

The answer on the next page is yet another example strongly showing the power of compound interest and the importance of getting started *now*.

Eggs in a Basket

Once you have your emergency fund of three to six months' expenses in place, you should begin to look at diversifying. The financial community calls this not putting all your eggs in one basket (probably because sometimes the financial community drops the basket). The concept of spreading your investments to avoid risk is very good. After you have your foundation laid, you should be careful not to leave all or the majority of your wealth in one institution or even in one type of investment. You should be careful not to attempt to get too fancy too soon. Unless you have at least $15,000, you can just keep it in your local bank or money market and be boring. But if you are saving actively and applying some of these principles, you very quickly will have more than that to watch over.

As of this writing, you are insured in FDIC banks up to

Ben and Arthur—both save at 12%—both save $2,000 per year. Ben starts at age 19 and stops. Arthur starts at age 27 and stops at 65.

AGE	BEN INVESTS		ARTHUR INVESTS	
19	2,000	2,240	0	0
20	2,000	4,749	0	0
21	2,000	7,558	0	0
22	2,000	10,706	0	0
23	2,000	14,230	0	0
24	2,000	18,178	0	0
25	2,000	22,599	0	0
26	2,000	27,551	0	0
27	0	30,857	2,000	2,240
28	0	34,560	2,000	4,749
29	0	38,708	2,000	7,558
30	0	43,352	2,000	10,706
31	0	48,554	2,000	14,230
32	0	54,381	2,000	18,178
33	0	60,907	2,000	22,599
34	0	68,216	2,000	27,551
35	0	76,802	2,000	33,097
36	0	85,570	2,000	39,309
37	0	95,383	2,000	46,266
38	0	107,339	2,000	54,058
39	0	120,220	2,000	62,785
40	0	134,646	2,000	72,559
41	0	150,804	2,000	83,506
42	0	168,900	2,000	95,767
43	0	189,168	2,000	109,499
44	0	211,869	2,000	124,879
45	0	237,293	2,000	142,104
46	0	265,768	2,000	161,396
47	0	297,660	2,000	183,004
48	0	333,379	2,000	207,204
49	0	373,385	2,000	234,308
50	0	418,191	2,000	264,665
51	0	468,374	2,000	298,665
52	0	524,579	2,000	336,745
53	0	587,528	2,000	379,394
54	0	658,032	2,000	427,161
55	0	736,995	2,000	480,660
56	0	825,435	2,000	540,579
57	0	924,487	2,000	607,688
58	0	1,035,425	2,000	682,851
59	0	1,159,676	2,000	767,033
60	0	1,298,837	2,000	861,317
61	0	1,454,698	2,000	966,915
62	0	1,629,261	2,000	1,085,185
63	0	1,824,773	2,000	1,217,647
64	0	2,043,746	2,000	1,366,005
65	**0**	**2,288,996**	**2,000**	**1,532,166**

. . . and he never caught up!
start now!!!!

$100,000 per individual, but you should not have all of your funds in one institution. If your FDIC bank fails—and many of them have—you will get your money. The problem is that it may be months or even years before the FDIC pays on the bank's insurance. So you should never bank in only one place. (Your banker will not like that advice!) You should also never have all your money in real estate or the stock market or money markets or in any one place. As your cash stash increases, you can get very sophisticated in your approach, but always remember that simplicity will usually win out over even the most learned advice when it comes to personal money management.

Attitude Is Everything

You must also be aware of your attitude as your cash increases. I have repeatedly said that "money is active," even in the spiritual sense. Consider again what Proverbs 21:20 says: "In the house of the wise are stores of choice food and oil, *but a foolish man devours all he has*" (emphasis added). You must be careful that you continue to own your money and that it never begins to own you as it grows. Larry Burkett, in his series called *How to Manage Your Money,* says, "Attitude is the only difference between saving and hoarding." Mike Murdock, another financial adviser, says, "Men will spend their health getting wealth. Then they gladly pay all they have earned to get their health back."

We are beginning to have some fun with this money

management "stuff." You can see the power that it can have in your finances as you take control instead of its having control of you. If you will heed the power of compound interest and have it work for you, you are ready to go from fun to fantasy in the next chapter.

Thoughts from Sharon . . .

Saving money . . . what peace that means to me.

When Dave and I were struggling several years ago, I didn't have any financial peace. I knew we had a small (very small) checking account. The IRAs and mutual funds we once had were all cashed in. Our income was no longer six-digit figures, but the average five digits. I began to feel scared and lost.

As we began to make our way back, we realized that saving money would play a major role in our household.

Yes, saving for a month or two may be difficult, but later it will become habit forming. It is so much fun to watch something grow. Why shouldn't it be a savings account, mutual fund, or IRA? You and your spouse have worked hard. You deserve the best. Begin now to save like there is no tomorrow.

To the husbands: The emergency fund is an investment in your marriage! Women feel more secure with that three to six months of expenses in the bank! And don't try to invest it in some fried pickle franchise. Leave it alone.

This step has brought such a comfort into our marriage. I hope it will do the same for you.

Peace Puppies

1. **Avoid "Stuffitis"—**The Worship of "Stuff"
2. **Plant Seeds—**Give Money Away to Worthy Causes
3. Develop Your Own **"Power over Purchase"**
4. **Find Where You Are Naturally Gifted—**Enjoy Your Work and Work Hard
5. **Live Substantially Below Your Income**
6. **Sacrifice Now** So You Can Have Peace Later
7. **You Can Always Spend More Than You Can Make**
8. **The Borrower Is the Servant to the Lender;** So Beware!
9. **Check Your Credit Report** at Least Once Every Two Years
10. **Handle Credit Report Corrections Yourself**
11. Realize That the Best Way for Delinquent Debt to Be Paid Is for You, Not Collectors, to **Control Your Financial Destiny**
12. **You Must Save Money** (the Power of Compound Interest)

CHAPTER ELEVEN

"KISS" Your Money

YEARS AGO, WHEN I worked daily in personal sales and later in training salespeople, I heard a saying. Most salespeople, especially when they are new, talk too much. They talk too much because of their desire to tell the client all the great things about their product or service. Many times a salesperson will talk his client out of the sale by overloading him with information he did not require to make a buying decision.

Keep It Simple, Stupid

Salespeople have to learn the art of being quiet at the appropriate time and of keeping their pitch simple. Because, with the exception of sales on technical products, people know whether they want a product or not after a reasonable amount of information has been presented to them. We were taught the KISS principle to avoid overcomplicating a presentation. KISS stands for "Keep It Simple, Stupid." We used this bit of comic relief to remind ourselves that it was counterproductive to overcomplicate things. More plainly, it is stupid to overcomplicate things that do not require it. The handling of money is no exception.

I am not calling anyone stupid, so please don't be offended, but you should remember this basic premise. People will lose thousands of dollars to prove they can invest with the sophisticates. I have had people come into my office who are completely broke, with negative monthly budgets and negative net worths, and then have them argue with me about the interest rate on a particular investment. I am continually amazed at all the broke financial geniuses. Our society has made it a sin to make unsophisticated, uncomplicated investments, but it is all right to have zero savings.

Well, I Know What I Am Doing

We brag about the investment we made or the great insurance program we have, and if Harry or Jill at work has a better one it is as if we didn't keep up with the Joneses. Most of us have gotten so focused on the tax advantages, the get-rich-quick scheme, or the sophistication of the investment that we forget to check it against common sense. There is something ridiculously glamorous about investing in something far away with a slick brochure that we don't quite understand. How about exotic bird partnerships with tax sheltered 200 percent returns? Don't you laugh; there are more absurd things out there that sell! Some say, "Well, I know what I am doing." How many times I have heard that. They are the ones about to fall the hardest.

> **Proverbs 17:12** *"Let a man meet a bear robbed of her cubs, rather than a fool in his folly."*

I Really Do Know What I Am Doing

I have a close friend who is a fairly wealthy doctor. I have seen his financial statements and know his business well. I talked with his business administrator at length and was told the physician's $2.5 million net worth would easily be over $5 million, and largely cash, were it not for one thing. He, like most of us, cannot resist a tax shelter or a great deal on a highly complicated, high-return investment. Real estate tax shelters, limited partnerships, bad stock tips, a horrible life insurance product, bad partnerships in other businesses, etc., have cost him millions of dollars in losses over the past ten years.

His administrator told me that if instead of wacky investments he had saved his cash at only 5 percent and just paid his taxes quietly, he would easily have double what he has now if not three times as much. In his search for financial sophistication, he has shot himself in the foot.

Yes, But That Is His Fault, or Is It?

We all do that only in smaller ways. This chapter will present a brief and basic overview of different investments and insurance and hopefully clarify the KISS principle of money. You must remember, though, that *no* investing in anything short of a savings account should be done until you have three to six months of expenses for an emergency fund. I am reminded of the old saying that the safest way to double your money is to fold it over once and put it in your pocket.

The Infamous Stock Market

First, let's look at the stock market. Individual stock purchases give you a tiny piece of ownership in a company. You have virtually no say in how the company is run. When you buy stocks you hope to get a return through the stock's increasing in value (purportedly because the company has done well) or through the company's giving its owners (stockholders) some of the profits through paid dividends.

For the part-time investor with his favorite stockbroker urging him on, studies have shown the average small portfolio has a poor return. The risk is astronomical for the income earner under $200,000 per year, and given this huge risk and poor offsetting return, individual stock purchases very seldom make sense for the typical family.

I know, I can hear you now, "But what about my grandpa who bought IBM stock for almost nothing in 1965 and got unbelievable returns?" For every IBM story there are hundreds of publicly traded companies in bankruptcy. Stories like IBM are legitimate, but they are the exception rather than the rule. The person who does not research stock for a living cannot hope to follow the necessary trends and measurements to accurately pick stocks. Even the normal stockbroker is taught more about selling than analyzing. Mark Twain summed it up well when he said, "October. This is one of the peculiarly dangerous months to speculate in stocks. The others are July, January, September, April, November, May, March, June, December, August, and February."

Bonds

Individual bond purchases have the same inherent problems and risk. The main difference here is that you are a creditor rather than an owner. When you purchase a bond, the company that issued it becomes your debtor. The income is usually fixed, but again the value or price of the bond will go up or down according to the performance of the company and prevailing interest rates. People who have portfolios and attempt to trade individual bonds on a part-time basis or through a stockbroker normally have very poor results.

If You Must

If you view yourself as a part-time wizard of the stock or bond market, I have a challenge for you. What if you *used no money* for this challenge? Instead you would have a hypothetical bank account with $200,000 in it and run this challenge for one year starting today. You would take the *Wall Street Journal* and tack it to your dart board. Next, you throw ten darts at it and invest $10,000 each (using $100,000) in the ten stocks closest to the darts. With the remaining $100,000 you would do your best job buying, selling, leveraging, and whatever you choose on the New York Stock Exchange for one year. At the end of a year, you would sell both hypothetical portfolios and see who did the best, you or the dart board. As a matter of fact, the *Wall Street Journal* runs a dart board contest against the pros and the darts win about 45 percent of the time. That's against the "best" stockbrokers. Real disheartening, isn't it?[1]

The dart board will beat most of us. If not, you should compare your rate of return to conservative investments, and you will probably find only a small difference. We get beat not because we are dumb, but simply because individual stocks selected without thorough investigation (anything short of full-time work) tend to do poorly on average.

Mutual Funds

Mutual funds are the best method of investing in the stock and bond markets for most people. Mutual funds are detailed in a later chapter.

Annuities

Annuities are simply savings accounts with a life insurance company or financial institution. They are not insured by the federal government, but they usually pay more than banks do on savings accounts. Life insurance companies are not as financially strong as they used to be, so you should be careful which one you choose. If they go broke, and a few have, you could lose your money—all of it.

Municipal Bonds

Tax-free municipal bonds are a popular investment for retirees, but I recommend the use of a mutual fund that invests in these. Cities and states are allowed to issue bonds (borrow money from the purchaser), and the interest that these bonds pay you is tax-free. Whatever income you get in the form of interest payments from these tax-free bonds has no federal income tax on it. If the bond pays 5 percent, and you are in a 30 percent income tax bracket, you would have to get 7.14 percent on a certificate of deposit or taxable bond to match it after taxes.

Rolling Dice or Commodities

The purchase of futures or commodities is foolish for the average person. Your chances of hitting the home run you want are better at the roulette table in Las Vegas, and I do not recommend either as sound investment strategy. No wireless cable, no unleaded gas, and no pork bellies!

Real Estate

Real estate investment beyond your personal home has good and bad points. You should never invest in real estate without having a substantial cash reserve in savings to smooth out the rough months. Responsibility for a bad rental property with no back-up savings has bankrupted many of my clients. On the other hand, real estate can be a great inflation hedge and can be a good vehicle for amassing wealth from several angles, including cash flow and tax benefits.

The mistake most novice real estate investors make is that they pay too much for properties. Deep, *deep* discounts should be your rule for rental property, and then you should borrow little or nothing on it. I have seen many people who bought real estate with little or no down payment and paid full appraisal for it. Then the payments are usually more than the rent or slightly less. When the payment is $750 and the rent is $800, you are losing money because of vacancy, maintenance, credit loss (bad tenants), and miscellaneous other drawbacks that the novice overlooks in his purchase.

Suddenly your glorious method to wealth becomes a white elephant. You owe so much that you cannot afford to sell it and it drains the other assets you've worked so hard to build. Real estate is a legitimate investment, but it should come only after you have accumulated lots of cash. So you should beware of brokers who know more about selling than they do about investments.

Simple Discipline Is the Key

If I sound negative about the investments I've mentioned, it is because I am. I have seen this glass bubble lure people to their financial deaths more times than I've seen their dreams of wealth come true. I have learned that the quickest way to get rich quick is *not* to get rich quick. Disciplined savings will outpace any investment scheme.

Insurance

Another area of complicated financial products is the area of insurance. Let me start out by saying that I'm a firm believer in low-cost insurance that provides full coverages.

The Bankruptcy Institute says that over 50 percent of consumer bankruptcies are the result of medical bills. If you do not have health insurance and can get it, you should do it now. It is financial suicide not to have health and disability insurance. If you have a family, I will go so far as to say it is irresponsible not to have health and disability insurance, unless you are prohibited from obtaining it. It is very expensive; as a matter of fact, it is often robbery. But then, you can lose a lifetime of work by not having it. You should carefully investigate and understand the options so that you know what your coverages are and then shop around.

Also you should do the same on homeowner's and auto insurance. These policies are more standardized. Most people have them and never use them. Here's one hint: if you have savings, you can raise your auto and homeowner's deductible to $500 or $1,000, and you will be amazed at the savings on your premium.

Life Insurance

Life insurance is an area where consumer confusion abounds. Few people understand the policies they own, but again it is irresponsible and poor planning to have no life insurance. The myriad of different insurance programs available boggles the normal consumer's mind.

Simply speaking, there are three general types of life insurance in the marketplace today: whole life, universal life, and term. While there are multitudes of variations on these themes, an understanding of these three fundamental types of life insurance will give you insight into the strengths and weaknesses of the programs now available.

Whole Life

Whole life is death coverage and a built-in savings program. Your premiums are high for the death protection and an unstated amount of the premium is going to build savings called cash value. The return on the savings program is extremely poor, usually around 3 percent. The industry calls the savings program cash value and tempts you into believing that it just appears there because you are a nice person. Wrong! You have paid more than needed to buy the death protection, and they have allocated some of the difference to a savings program that pays a poor rate of return.

Let's pick on Joe some more. Joe buys a whole life policy with a face amount of $70,000, pays on it for ten years, and builds up a cash value of $8,000. Then something happens to poor Joe. What does the company pay to Sue and the kids? Answer: $70,000. If Joe has been paying too much for insurance for ten years so that he can build cash value, what happened to the cash value (saving at 3 percent) at Joe's death? His insurance company keeps it. Sounds fair to me! Ha! I am strongly against whole life life insurance because I don't like the system under which you are saving—and it is expensive.

Universal or Variable Life

Universal life is the updated version of whole life. When the insurance companies began to realize that consumers were catching on to whole life, they tried to make it more palatable. Universal life usually pays a better interest rate on the savings program, and most now allow your beneficiary (spouse) to get the face amount *plus* the savings account (cash value) at death.

So what is wrong with this? The cost of the pure insurance inside the plan is normally high, and therefore less of your premium is going to savings. The savings, while it does better than whole life, seldom reaches the "projected rate" you were sold of 9 or 10 percent. If we judge the savings portion as we judge a mutual fund—on its track record—it will not even stack up to a certificate of deposit. So what we end up with is expensive insurance and a mediocre savings program. Why would a company out for profit ever offer to help you save money if it did not make a profit from doing so? Again, beware of any life insurance that has a built-in savings program.

Term & Level Term

Term life insurance is pure insurance. You are getting no savings program, which is good news after looking at the last two. Term is like your auto or homeowner's insurance. If the event occurs, the insurance company pays. Simple, no bells, no whistles. I, like most competent financial planners, recommend the purchase of low-cost level term insurance for ten to twenty years (guaranteed renewable) and then invest the difference. What difference? The premium for level term will run as much as 70 percent less than the above-mentioned types, and you should put yourself in a forced savings program for that saved amount.

A Home Run

One interesting approach is to open an Individual Retirement Account (IRA) on a monthly checking draw for the amount you save and have it sent to a mutual fund with a long, good, track record. (More on this in the next chapter.) I have reviewed many life policies, and I have never seen one that would beat buying term and investing the premium savings in an IRA in a 12 percent average annual return mutual fund. So you must be wary of life insurance agents. The commissions are higher on universal life and whole life than on term and for obvious reasons: the company makes more profit on those products.

The Worst

There is one other type of insurance that we buy that should be discussed here, namely credit life or mortgage life insurance. The purpose of this insurance is to pay off your mortgage or a particular loan if you die. When you bought that stereo on ninety-days-same-as-cash, didn't pay it off in ninety days, and converted the loan to payments, you were probably sold credit life.

Credit life is the most expensive, horrible life insurance there is, short of having no insurance. A lender may require you to have life insurance adequate to pay off the loan in the event of your death, but he cannot require you to buy it from him, so don't. Finance companies make almost as much on insurance premiums as on interest, and the managers are often paid bonuses for selling you the overpriced garbage. The typical credit life policy is ninety to two hundred times more expensive than level term.[2] The credit card industry makes an extra $1 billion a year on life insurance to cover your balance.[3] Trashy, trashy, trashy!

Mortgage life is not quite as high, but you can usually buy a level term policy of the same face amount for less than half the cost of mortgage life insurance. Here's the simple rule: you do not buy insurance from a lender.

Just "KISS" the Money

You may be thinking that I am some sort of doomsayer or that I never had a positive thought in my life. Well, it is not that grim. I am simply stating the facts on these investments and insurance products. Very gradually, we have let different changes in financial philosophy creep into our lives. We have to stop being enamored by the sheer complexity of these horrible investments.

We have to use the "Keep It Simple, Stupid" rule of investment. Simple is better, and I know that sounds un-American, but just consider the common sense of it. You should never invest in anything you do not understand thoroughly, and by that I mean upside down, frontward, and backward. If you cannot explain it to someone else, you should not buy it or invest in it. One in five Americans will be victimized by a financial scam in their lifetime.[4] Again, you should never invest in anything you do not thoroughly understand—except possibly a spouse.

Thoughts from Sharon . . .

Investing money now is what will make you wealthy later in life. I have heard this over and over. As an adult, I'm beginning to understand that concept better.

Over the years, Dave and I have invested money in a lot of different areas. Dave, being the numbers man, knows more about investing than I do. This is an area of his work that he loves. Because he has done well at this, I have depended on his knowledge to make the best choices.

Yes, I know all about the types of insurance and mutual funds we have. After all, Dave's rule is "Don't buy unless you completely understand it." I hope your spouse explains the meaning of your investments to you. If not, just ask. Most people love to talk about the great deal they got.

Peace Puppies

1. **Avoid "Stuffitis"—**The Worship of "Stuff"
2. **Plant Seeds—**Give Money Away to Worthy Causes
3. Develop Your Own **"Power over Purchase"**
4. **Find Where You Are Naturally Gifted—**Enjoy Your Work and Work Hard
5. **Live Substantially Below Your Income**
6. **Sacrifice Now** So You Can Have Peace Later
7. **You Can Always Spend More Than You Can Make**
8. **The Borrower Is the Servant to the Lender;** So Beware!
9. **Check Your Credit Report** at Least Once Every Two Years
10. **Handle Credit Report Corrections Yourself**
11. Realize That the Best Way for Delinquent Debt to Be Paid Is for You, Not Collectors, to **Control Your Financial Destiny**
12. **You Must Save Money** (the Power of Compound Interest)
13. Use the **"Keep It Simple, Stupid"** Rule of Investing

CHAPTER TWELVE

Of Mice and Mutual Funds

WHAT GOES UP faster than the price of a new Cadillac? What has more inflation-beating power than a speeding Consumer Price Index? What is able to leap even the ever increasing price of a postage stamp in a single bound? It's a bird! No, it's a plane! No, it's Super Fund, that's what! The huge increase in sales of mutual funds has made them the topic around the investment barber shop for the last decade. Why? Well, I'm going to tell you and show you.

The Hottest Thing Since Microwaves

Mutual funds are hopping. There are currently over 100 funds managing more than $1,000,000,000 ($1 billion) each, and two funds are now over $20 billion each, according to a recent *USA Today* listing.[1] These funds offer the common man access to things to which we aren't usually entitled, like good diversification and good management. Thousands of people invest each week because many of the funds will allow as little as $25 to $50 per month or as little as $250 to $500 one-time investments. You and I can get in, but do we want to? You should remember our rule by now: You never put money in anything you don't understand. So it is time to understand.

You Have to Beat the Monster

The monster is inflation. The Consumer Price Index (CPI) is our best measure of inflation. Many argue, and accurately so, that the CPI is a lousy index, but it is the best measure of inflation that we have, so we will use it. In the last fifty years inflation has averaged 4.35 percent per year;[2] if we don't save long term at a faster rate, we will retire with a lot of money that won't buy much. A postage stamp sold for six cents in 1970 and by 2002 sold for thirty-four cents, a 5.57 percent increase per year on average. If you want to mail those grandkids some gifts, you must save at a rate of return faster than inflation. Stock type mutual funds have done that in the past and so as people understand them more and more they are putting more and more money in them.

That Good Ole Mixin' Bowl

Okay, okay. What is all the fuss about and just what is a confounded mutual fund anyway? Well I'm glad you asked, because even though I got a finance degree from a major college, for many years I couldn't tell you what a mutual fund was, much less how it works. Most people get lucky and get into a good fund without knowing what they bought, but not you and me, not anymore. Now I only invest in things I understand.

Mutual funds are just what the name implies. You, me, and a few other people put money together in a fund; thus, we have mutually funded this fund. You can visualize that big ole mixin' bowl in your mom's kitchen. If you set that bowl in the middle of the table, I'll put in my $100 and you put in your $1,000 and some others can put in their $500 and so on. Now we have a fund that was *mutually funded.*

So what do we do with this money? What is done with the money is determined by the *fund objective,* a neat term that means our goal. If our fund is a growth stock fund, our fund manager will buy growth stocks. If our fund is a corporate bond fund, our fund manager will buy corporate bonds. If our fund is an international stock fund, our fund manager will buy what? You got it! International stocks. See, this isn't hard, is it?

George of the Jungle

Let's imagine George is our fund manager. We picked our fund because of its fine management track record. Our fund is a growth stock fund so George took the money out of our mixin' bowl and bought the stock of companies that are growing. Like most growth funds he bought one hundred to two hundred different growing companies' stocks. So now we own stock in companies that make everything from tires to toothpaste, flour to fire alarms, carpet to Coke, and even banks to barns (one stinks and I'll let you guess which one).

Well, I have great news: all these companies have been making a killing off you all these years and now you own a little piece of each one. Isn't that fun? You bet it is, and here is why. What is inflation made up of? All those products we buy every day. So if we own a little piece of those companies that make those products, we are virtually guaranteed to stay ahead of inflation, and we get a little of the money back those companies have been getting off us for years.

Back to George. Why did we pick this fund? Because it has a fine management track record. What is that? That means George and his team have a record of keeping good growing stocks and low expenses. Out of the one hundred to two hundred stocks George picked, most of them went up in value. If I had put my money in ten years ago, it would have made me more than 12 percent on the average year. That is a good track record.

George's Nerd Team

George is kind of like Santa. Santa gets all the glory, but the elves do the real work. The way George knows which stock is a good one and which is a bad one is his Bat Phone rings and someone tells him which stocks to buy and which to sell. That someone at the other end is one of George's Nerd team. George has a whole team of Nerds called stock analysts (sorry, guys) and their job is to know more about that stock than any other Nerd on the planet. If your job is restaurant Nerd, than you know everything about restaurants. You eat at them and judge their service and prices. You watch sales of certain locations and regions. You visit the corporate offices. You go to restaurant industry meetings. You know if they have failing locations and what their growth is. You know everything there is to know about restaurants and about that particular company because that is your full-time job.

It is very safe to say George's nerds are way ahead of you, me, or even your stockbroker in knowing what is happening with a particular industry or company. They know when to buy and when to sell that stock. You have to keep in mind that George has a Nerd and a Nerd's assistant assigned to each industry and many times even to individual companies. If George's Nerds are right, then George has bought the right stocks and his fund has made money, good money, over the last ten or fifteen years. So I can feel comfortable buying into this mutual fund.

So our mom's ole mixin' bowl is now full of one hundred to two hundred stocks of good growth companies picked by the able hands of the best Nerds in the business. You and I own our proportional share of the fund based on what we put in. Then one day we read in the newspaper that the stock market dropped today and we start to wonder, "Is this safe?"

Guarantees Are for Children

If you grow up in a safe environment with love and nurturing, then you make a pretty decent adult. If you don't, then you have to learn how to trust everyone, including yourself. If you were lucky enough to grow up safe, then you have had some guarantees; but as you became a teenager you went out a little in that cold, cruel world and found it isn't always safe. As we grow up and become functioning adults, we spend all our time in that cold, cruel world. Soon we learn that the only guarantees are our Lord and our own ability to kill something and drag it home. If we keep being adults, we find that we would have it no other way. The lion at the zoo is a pitiful sight—the king of beasts is eating processed food. You can see deep down in his soulful eyes that he misses the thrill of the hunt.

Any of you who want a guarantee on your money need to understand that you are paying the same price as the lion. Over the last sixty years inflation has averaged 4.07 percent per year and those precious CDs have averaged 4.36 percent.[3] So if your money is in CDs, you have virtually treaded water. If you save for long-term goals like retirement and only tread water, you have put yourself on a pauper's budget and you better develop a taste for Alpo burgers or Purina prime rib. Just like the lion, you have a guarantee, but the price is too high.

There are two main kinds of investment risk—the risk

of the loss of principal, which is the money put in, and the risk that inflation will beat you to the bank and take your money. Most people forget about inflation and look for guarantees. And after taxes and inflation you get your guarantee, a guaranteed net loss in purchasing power.

The Great American Dream

If you own a home, are you guaranteed by the government that it will never go down in value? No. Then why were you so comfortable in buying that home? You know the track record. You know that in most parts of the United States, single family homes go up in value. Some years they go up a bunch (inflation) and some years they go up a little and even some years they might go down a little, but we never worry because we know if we wait just a little while they will go up again. On the average, the single family home increases in value over the five- to ten-year haul; that is real estate's track record. We get our comfort from a track record, not a guarantee. Mutual funds can be selected the same way.

I own a growth and income fund that has not had a down year in over fifteen years. This particular fund has a track record over sixty years, back to the Great Depression, and has an average annual return of over 12 percent over sixty years. I feel comfortable with that track record. There are hundreds of funds with great ten- to fifteen-year track records; a good five-year track record is a minimum. *Lipper Analytical* says that over 80 percent of equity (stock) mutual funds have averaged over 12 percent per year in the last fifteen years.[4]

Mutual funds are never short-term investments. If you cannot leave money alone at least five years, then you should not invest. Ibbotson's yearbook, a reference on most mutual fund brokers' desks, advises that if you had invested on the short term, just one year, in small company stocks you would have lost money twenty of the last sixty-nine years. However, by leaving your investment alone in any possible ten-year period in the last sixty-nine years, you would have made money 97 percent of the time and would have averaged over 12 percent per year.[5]

The Great Ca-Boom

Can mutual funds fail? Sure, they can, but to date no stock mutual funds have because all the one hundred to two hundred companies would have to go broke. If the top one hundred to two hundred companies in America go broke, your CD isn't safe either because our whole economy will have collapsed. I just can't do a Chicken Little imitation even though I have been through personal trials that no one should have to endure.

That Candy Store Feeling

Some of you may feel like the kid outside the candy store with his nose fogging the glass, just wanting a taste. The only problem is how to best spend that one dollar your daddy gave you. In other words, how do you pick a mutual fund?

First let's discuss the kinds of funds I would pick if I were you. Remember that the type of fund tells us what the money in the ole mixin' bowl is used to purchase. I suggest for beginners with under $10,000 that you pick a growth and income fund. This type of fund is calm, with not much fluctuation, which will not scare the beginner. It buys some growth stocks and some large-company stocks that don't grow much but pay an income called dividends.

A Proper Portfolio

"A proper portfolio" sounds official, doesn't it? If you have over $10,000 to invest, I would spread it across four of these fund types. But, with over $50,000 to invest I would find two or three mutual funds of each type so that you would own eight to twelve funds with one hundred to two hundred stocks in each one. That is spreading your risk, or diversification.

The calmest type I use is the balanced fund. The balanced fund is invested in a balance of small-company stocks for growth, large-company stocks for growth and income, and even some bonds.

Next up the list is our beginner's friend, the growth and income fund, which as we just said has some small-company and some large-company stock to create some growth and some income.

Getting slightly wilder is the growth fund, which concentrates solely on long-term growth and will have small-company stocks and a few of the growing large-company stocks.

The international fund should be in each portfolio because when the good ole U.S. isn't doing so hot some years, many of the companies overseas are. International will be more wild, but it will have better returns over the long haul. And you need to remember that only 25 percent goes into this category.

The roller coaster of the bunch is the aggressive growth fund or small-company fund. This fund buys smaller, more aggressive company stocks so it makes it big or busts it big, but on the average the returns on the quality funds have been very good. I own one aggressive growth fund that has averaged over 19 percent per year over ten years, but you have to hold on for the ride.

If you are more calm, you can invest in balanced, growth and income, growth, and international. If you want to be more aggressive then you should lean toward growth and income, growth, international, and aggressive growth.

How to Find George

George is not as difficult to find as Waldo. George is not hiding. Mutual funds will help you find them and give you more information than you want or need, and then you can get confused and give up. So here is how to pick a fund. I use four criteria—performance, family, roller coaster, and expenses.

"P" Is for Performance

Performance track record is the most important criterion I use. How much money did George make? You are looking for average annual return compounded over at least five years. You don't buy baby funds. If the fund is only three years old, it still needs diapers. I want one that is old enough to have seen some hard times; hard times make you wise. How did the fund do after black October 1987? If it has a great fifteen-year track record that encompasses that date, you have a good fund. When comparing track records or rates of return, you should compare within fund types. You can't compare a balanced fund to an aggressive growth fund. (You need to compare apples to apples and oranges to oranges.)

We Are Family

The next area I look at is the family of funds. Each family of funds contains several funds of many types. Does this family do well in most of its funds? Have they been around awhile as a family? Many families now have replaced George with a team of managers. So four or five people make the decisions, not just one, in any given fund. The benefit to this team approach to management is that if one dies or leaves the fund all the knowledge doesn't go with that person. If one superstar George manages the fund, then the fund could falter if he quit. I like the diversification of management.

Whee! Whee!

Roller coasters are fun if they are safe. So when comparing two funds of the same type, you should compare how high are the mountains and how low are the valleys. The wildness measurement is called a beta. The beta measures statistically the volatility of a fund's past. A beta of 1.0 is the exact wildness of the top five hundred stocks called the Standard & Poor Index. The stock market moves at 1.0, so if your fund is more than 1.0 beta it is wilder than the overall market. Almost all aggressive growth funds will have over 1.0 betas like 1.5 or 1.7. If your fund's beta is less than 1.0, then it is calmer than the overall stock market. Most balanced funds and growth and income funds will be below 1.0, at betas like .90 or .80.

You Cheapskate You

The last criterion I use to select a fund is expenses. This is the most overworked and overrated criterion out there. Too many times someone will tell you how low his expense ratio is, just as that blind date in high school with the great personality always turned out to be seriously ugly. The correct way to judge expenses is to look in the fund prospectus—the paperwork—for a simple chart showing average expenses per thousand dollars invested. This figure reflects all expenses, including commissions. You should look at the ten-year average and compare again among the same types of funds. If the average is $20, then the ratio per thousand over ten years is 2 percent.

To Load or Not to Load?

I am frequently asked whether you should buy a fund with a load, which is a commission, or a no-load fund. My answer is either. You should look at all the criteria listed above and at the expense averages. I have seen many no-load (no-commission) funds with higher expenses than ones that include commissions, so don't assume that no-load means cheaper or better. There is no credible research that shows load funds or no-load funds do better all the time. There are lousy and great of each, so don't tell me about some magazine that sells ads to no-load funds and that said buy only no-loads. (Can you say conflict of interest?) And don't tell me that your broker says that loaded funds are always better either.

The biggest mistake people make is putting too much emphasis on expenses as a criterion. If my expenses were .5 percent higher (a lot), but my fund has a performance track record of 16 percent on the average and yours averages 9 percent, who wins? I do. I eat prime rib and you eat hamburger at retirement, but your expenses were lower.

Funding Those Golden Rocking Chairs

Once you have saved your emergency fund that we talked about in previous chapters, and you are saving to pay cash for purchases, then you should start to load up on wealth-building like retirement. But no one is. A recent *USA Today*/CNN/Gallup poll stated that only 44 percent of Americans are preparing for retirement.[6] I guess that means the other 56 percent are counting on Social Insecurity. In an online survey, Consolidated Credit Counseling Services found that 50 percent of participants do not have a savings account and 92 percent do not have an emergency fund for three months of living expenses.[7] A survey by benefits consulting firm Watson Wyatt found that about half of the large companies still have traditional pensions—down from 89 percent in 1985. Workers across the country have been shortchanged by almost $200 million per year because hundreds of companies have done away with traditional pension plans.[8] This trend means it is up to you! Santa Claus is not going to fund your retirement, so you will have to. So what is the best way to save money?

A Government Gift?

Billionaire J. Paul Getty says that one of the keys to building wealth is not to pay taxes on money until you use it. So you shouldn't pay taxes on retirement dollars until you use them. You should always invest long term with pretax dollars. What if I gave you $2,000 each year and these were the conditions: You can earn all the interest you want on that $2,000—and keep it—but you have to give the $2,000 for each year back to me when you are seventy years old. If you were thirty-five years old and we did that for thirty-five years at 12 percent, you would have $863,326. You do have to give me back $2,000 × 35 years or $70,000, but you still net $793,326. If you save $6,700 per year in a pretax investment like a 401(k) or SEPP (Simplified Employee Pension Plan), the above scenario would have occurred. If you bring that $6,700 per year home, it turns into $4,700 by the time Uncle Congress gets his greedy cut, so $2,000 of that money is Uncle Congress's—which, if we invest pretax, we get to keep for free all those years. What a deal!

I have heard the ridiculous pitch that it is better to pay your taxes today because tax rates may be higher by the time you get to retirement. The only people who believe that argument do not understand the power of the present value of dollars or are life insurance salesmen.

IRAs, 401(k)s, 403(b)s, and UFOs

The government puts a number or initial on just about everything. Our mission, should we decide to accept it, is to retire with dignity; to do that we must decode the secret government code. An IRA is not the Irish Republican Army's mutual fund, nor is it a bank-only product. An IRA is an individual retirement account that can be invested in a bunch of different places, and probably the worst place is in the bank. Mutual funds as outlined above are what I use to fund all my retirement planning. An IRA is not a product sold at banks; it is merely the way the IRS treats a particular investment. Want to hear a million-dollar word? Roth. The Roth IRA in a good mutual fund could save you more than a million dollars in taxes. If a thirty-year-old saves $500 per month in a retirement account until he is seventy years old he will, at 12 percent average, have almost $6,000,000. If you are young you should always fund a Roth IRA first (unless you get a match at work) because the Roth grows completely *tax free*. What that means is $6 million in a 401(k) would pay almost $2 million in taxes, whereas if the same were saved in a Roth the whole $6 million would be *tax free*, a $2 million savings! See your CPA for up-to-date tax info and see if you qualify for a Roth.

Get a Real Job

For those of you who are self-employed like me and who feel the world wants to know when you'll get "a real job," the SEPP is available. The Simplified Employee Pension Plan is not simple, but you will prevail. Again, it is a tax-deductible, tax-deferred plan for small-business people to save money. Without becoming a tax manual, I can't give all the details, but if you are self-employed, you need a SEPP. Your CPA or mutual fund broker can help.

The Real People

Those of you with real jobs with medium to large companies probably have a 401(k) available for retirement through payroll deductions. This retirement plan gives you nothing unless you put in something, so for goodness' sake you need to put something in. According to *Fortune* magazine, the research group Public Agenda estimates that almost 75 percent of Americans fear they aren't saving enough for retirement,[9] but only a few are willing to do something about it. After you get out of debt, it is easy to put your money into your 401(k). *Business Week* reports that only one in four people participate in their 401(k) and only 39 percent know where their money is invested.[10] That's double dumb.

The typical 401(k) plan will offer four to ten options. You should not invest in the guaranteed investment contracts or bonds. I would choose the mutual fund options outlined above and select them using the principles outlined above. Growth, growth and income, international, and aggressive growth should be your selections, with your money distributed evenly if they all have good five-year or longer track records. If you don't have good options, you should complain to your human resources manager because he or she is likely in the plan too and knows your options stink.

You should never borrow on your 401(k) plan. As I read some of the stupid articles out there, all the nightmares in my office of clients in trouble because of 401(k) borrowing come back to haunt me. First of all, you are unplugging good 12 percent mutual funds to have the joy of paying yourself 5 or 6 percent interest. If you leave the company, you had better get ready to repay the loan, or it will be considered an early withdrawal with big-time penalties and taxes. Do you think that will never happen to you? Have you ever heard of downsizing?

You should contribute to your 401(k) plan whether or not your employer matches. It is a great pretax, tax-deferred investment; if your employer matches some or all of your contribution, then that amount is gravy. A 50 percent match is a 50 percent return on investment if your mutual fund does nothing. That's a great deal!!

The 403(b) is for nonprofit organizations, hospitals, school systems, and the like, and is virtually the same thing as the 401(k). If one is available to you, you should fund it.

The point is that regardless of the number or initials of the plan, you should do all the pretax, tax-deferred investing you can do for retirement.

How Fast They Grow

It seems like only yesterday when we brought our first child home from the hospital. Then it seemed like just a couple of days had passed before she was toddling around the kitchen, using her hands to feel her way around. No more than a month later, I walked into the kitchen and there was my toddler, now nine years old, cooking. My oh my, time goes so fast. At this rate in a couple more days she will be wanting something as absurd as help with college.

How should you save for college? The answer is never in a life insurance policy and never in savings bonds, which don't average as much as tuition inflation. I suggest saving for college in good, long track record mutual funds. The best way I know to save in a mutual fund is the ESA, the Educational Savings Account. The ESA is nicknamed The Education IRA because it grows *tax free* if used for education. It is very flexible and you, the parent, are in control of the investments. The neat thing is if you started when the child was a baby, saving $2,000 per year, you would have over $130,000 when the child reaches age eighteen if the mutual fund averaged 12 percent. Now think with me: eighteen years at $2,000 is only $36,000 you put in, so almost $100,000 is growth that grew *tax free*.

The 529 plans are also growing in popularity and flexibility. You should usually do the ESA first and then move in the 529 direction. They also grow tax free; but you have much less control of the investments in most plans, so I would learn a lot about the particular plan before investing. See your CPA or mutual fund professional to see which you qualify for. Also, never do prepaid tuition because all you are making on your money is the inflation rate of tuition, which is about 7 percent per year.

Investing Isn't So Hard, Is It?

Learning to invest in mutual funds may have seemed like learning a foreign language. Now hopefully you have a better understanding, and I am sure you also know by now that I am excited about mutual funds. They are not perfect, but neither is life. I own several funds and I hope you begin your journey into the land of better returns. You just need to remember to establish the emergency fund, never invest in anything you don't understand, and never invest in something if the risk robs your or your spouse's peace. Life is too short for greed to keep you awake. I urge you to learn about these funds because knowledge will remove fear!

Disclaimer: The figures regarding mutual funds reflect past results and are not predictive of future results. Neither the publisher nor author of this material is associated with any mutual fund company. This book is not a sales promotion for mutual funds nor is it an inducement to buy.

Thoughts from Sharon . . .

What do mutual funds mean to me? When I think of mutual funds and investments, I picture a river, small and narrow. After several years of heavy rain and miles of flowing water, the river has grown. Eventually this small river becomes a lake.

Since the lake is continuously fed, the fast running water turns into a huge peaceful pool of water. And if the water has nowhere to go, it can only get deeper and wider.

The flow of money invested in mutual funds works the same way. It continues to grow and eventually will overflow its banks.

Peace Puppies

1. **Avoid "Stuffitis"—**The Worship of "Stuff"
2. **Plant Seeds—**Give Money Away to Worthy Causes
3. Develop Your Own **"Power over Purchase"**
4. **Find Where You Are Naturally Gifted—**Enjoy Your Work and Work Hard
5. **Live Substantially Below Your Income**
6. **Sacrifice Now** So You Can Have Peace Later
7. **You Can Always Spend More Than You Can Make**
8. **The Borrower Is the Servant to the Lender;** So Beware!
9. **Check Your Credit Report** at Least Once Every Two Years
10. **Handle Credit Report Corrections Yourself**
11. Realize That the Best Way for Delinquent Debt to Be Paid Is for You, Not Collectors, to **Control Your Financial Destiny**
12. **You Must Save Money** (the Power of Compound Interest)
13. Use the **"Keep It Simple, Stupid"** Rule of Investing
14. **Only People Who Like Dog Food Don't Save for Retirement**
15. **Always Save with Pretax Dollars—**It Is the Best Deal the Government Gives You

CHAPTER THIRTEEN

Buy Only Big, Big Bargains

FUN, FUN, FUN, *fun!* That is what getting a great buy on something of good quality that you really need is—just plain *f-u-n.* This chapter covers the most fun of these basic principles. After all that discipline, let's go and get a "steal" of a deal!

You must understand three essential things to hunt big game, and "big bargains": you must learn to negotiate; you must learn where to find bargains; and you must have patience. We will discuss each one in detail.

Everything, I Mean Everything

First, you must learn to negotiate *everything.* Everything you buy is negotiable at some time, at some place, and you must find it. The days of impulse buying are over, and the days of negotiation are in for the people who want to get control of their financial lives.

Most people are very anticonfrontational by nature. Most of us, even the boisterous and outgoing, do not want head-to-head confrontation. If you understand that people do not want to meet head-on, it will aid you in your negotiations. If you will approach your purchase looking for a way to win for everyone, you will buy things very cheaply. If someone needs to sell very badly, you have helped him by making that purchase. But you must win too, and your winning can occur in the area of price or terms.

The Way to Do Win-Win

In *Getting to Yes,* Roger Fisher and William Ury of the Harvard Negotiation Project tell a classic story illustrating how everyone can win in a negotiation: "There were once two elderly ladies who had one orange between them which they were negotiating for. After a lengthy discussion these two ladies could not come up with a solution except to split the difference, so they cut the orange in half, each taking one half. One lady proceeded to peel the orange and use the peel for baking a cake, while the other peeled her half and ate the fruit."[1]

If the two had spent time, through good communication, finding out what the other's needs were for the orange, they both could have had the whole orange, and neither would have been the lesser. The point of the story is that if you bring creativity and communication to your purchases you can make excellent buys and help people in the process.

I Mean Everything

You must negotiate with everyone. Two major pizza chains in our area are competing aggressively for their share of the market. My family prefers the taste of one brand better, but the other brand runs better advertised specials. My wife determined to get the brand we wanted at the other's price, so when she called to place the order she told our brand they would have to match the other brand's price if they wanted the business. At first they did not want to, because there was a good bit of price difference, but when my wife explained that she would simply call the other brand and place an order, they gave us the good pizza at the good price. Our family does this just for the fun of it.

I do not buy a car stereo from the showroom floor. I want them to bring the one from the back with a small scratch, and I will save $200. I buy kitchen appliances, cars, clothes—everything—at discount, simply because I have the nerve to ask.

Everyone Else Does

If you have ever visited any foreign country you know that haggling in the marketplace is a way of life for all the rest of the world. But not us. Oh, no! We have to go to the shining shopping mall and pay full retail with markup plus, and we charge it at 18 percent interest or we are not happy. It is time to change! We must start today to do things differently.

Trade

Another method of negotiating is to trade. You can trade goods or services you have for others' goods or services if you will just remember to ask. I have traded two .22 rifles for which I paid $10 apiece and had never shot in five years for $100 worth of landscaping. I have traded stock for real estate and land for houses, etc. I have traded a small consulting job of two hours for new carpet (top quality) in my den. Young couples trying to get started can trade painting or yard work for rent or for a down payment on a first home. If you will just think, you will find you have services and goods of value that someone else needs, and you have a potential trade.

The Basics

When you begin this process of negotiating, you should stay calm and use some basic principles. While negotiating can be a very complex and detailed science, in normal consumer purchases you will meet only about 2 percent of the people who understand and implement what I call the "lucky seven" basic principles of negotiating.

1. *Always Tell the Truth*

There is never enough money to be made or lost on a deal to warrant a lack of integrity. As a society we seem to have lost this simple and yet far-reaching and profound principle.

2. *Use the Power of Cash*

Now that you have saved some money from the last few chapters, you can explore just how much negotiating power that has given you. Not only have you saved money and used compound interest in your favor, but you also get to see the real benefit. People get silly when they see cash—not a check or bank note—*cash*. There is something highly emotional about flashing cash when making a purchase. People react to the surety and the instancy of *cash*.

If you are buying a car from an individual, and you have thoroughly checked it out and are ready to make an offer, do it in cash. If you will count out slowly and dramatically $5,000 in $100 bills on his trunk lid, you can often buy that car at that price rather than his asking price of $7,000. If you are buying a $2,000 computer, you should use cash as a visual example of what you will pay for it; you will get a discount. I have a friend who buys foreclosure real estate with cash in small denominations. He gets a $19 briefcase with loud latches, fills it with $50,000 in $20 bills, opens it with great fanfare, and says, "Here is my offer, $50,000." You would not believe the stories he tells of people's reactions, but he gets great buys on real estate.

3. Understand and Use "Walk Away Power"

You must be prepared to walk away and not make the purchase. If the seller senses—and he can—that you are committed to that purchase, you will receive no discounts. Sometimes this is not a bluff, and you must simply walk away to buy another day. You cannot be committed to someone's product or service before the transaction is complete. I know of irreputable real estate people who wait until you sit down to sign the closing papers on the house and then change the deal. They figure no one will back out at that point, and they are usually right.

4. Shut Up

You talk too much. We all talk too much. When faced with a purchase, we sense the inherent confrontation, get nervous, and talk too much. Even the big-time pro negotiators do this. If you will simply shut up, people will talk themselves *out* of more than you will ever talk them into. You just need to make small comments and let the other person rattle. For example, you can say, "Joe, it seems that your price is possibly too high." Then you shut up and see just how far he will talk *himself* down on the price.

5. "That Is Not Good Enough"

It is said that Henry Kissinger once asked a member of his staff to research a particular subject and write a paper on it. After six months of research and writing, the staffer set the document on his desk for Kissinger's approval. The staffer received the report back the next day with "You'll have to do better. This is not good enough" written across it. So the staffer spent another three months doing further research and resubmitted his report, only to have it returned the next day with the same words across it.

Once again the staffer went to work and spent another month fine-tuning his findings. This time out of exasperation he personally took the paper to Kissinger, telling him there was positively nothing further to be learned on this subject on planet Earth. Kissinger then responded, "Good, *now* I will read it. . . ." Kissinger knew that everyone has more room to expand or reduce anything.[2]

The same principle holds true when negotiating. When the price is given, you should reply, "That is not good enough. What can you really do?" You will see the price drop, sometimes lower than you would have offered. Instead of your giving a lower offer, you should try using this approach—and see what happens.

6. *Good Guy—Bad Guy*

Your wife or husband, who is not with you, should always seem mean to the other side. "My wife would kill me if I took that price" or "You know, my husband doesn't like it if I come home with a new dress if I didn't get a good buy." You should always use this—and you should also be very aware that it is used against you by retailers. They call it "position selling."

I am sure you have heard a salesman say, "Let me check with my manager on your offer." When he comes back, he says the manager—who has one eye in the center of his head and foams at the mouth—just won't go along with your offer, but he will let you buy today, and today only, at blank price. You should not let them use it on you. Please note: when you use this technique and make an offer to buy, you must tell the truth and be willing to buy at that price.

7. "If I . . ."—Give, But Take

When you reach a point that you must give up something, you need to be sure you take something while you are doing that. You should say "If I . . . give you $2,500 for that entertainment center, then you have to throw in the delivery (or something) and the sales tax at no extra charge." You must not just give. Instead, you should always make your giving contingent upon your receiving something else in return.

Does this conversation seem familiar to you? "Mommy, I want that toy." "Sure, son, if you clean up your room." Works everywhere, doesn't it?

Now Do It

That is the "lucky seven." It is fun to negotiate, and I have used small-dollar examples. I have, however, used these same principles on million-dollar real estate deals, and they still work. You must look for the way everyone can win and then begin to explore and ask questions. Keep your eyes open and you can have a lot of fun with this.

You will never get peace in your finances until you learn to buy at bargains and to do that you must employ these basic negotiating principles:

1. Always tell the truth.
2. Use the power of cash.
3. Understand and use "walk away power."
4. Shut up.
5. "That is not good enough."
6. Good guy—bad guy.
7. "If I . . ."—give, but take.

The Hunt

The second element you must understand to get great buys is that deals are like buried treasure. You must hunt far and wide for that really good deal. To purchase an $18,000 car for $11,000, you do not look in the dealer ads in the newspaper. Deals like that do not get advertised by dealers. They buy them and sell to you at retail.

Individuals

Individuals are a good source for great buys. They have a reason to sell now and are seldom motivated by profit, but more by a need to turn that item into something they need, like cash. The "power of cash" is particularly strong with individuals selling slightly used items they no longer want or need. They are more likely to have fewer defenses to basic negotiating and feel the pressure of your walking away much more than a retail business.

I do not buy cars from dealers. You are welcome to do so—after all, someone has to buy new cars—but I will never again pay retail for an item that depreciates by huge percentages in the first few years. *Kiplinger's Personal Money Management* magazine's yearly survey of automobiles reveals that the typical new car will lose 60 to 70 percent of its sticker price in just four years.[3]

I have heard the pitch that the luxury cars of Brand X and Brand Z hold their sticker price better than the others, but one is merely lousy and the other is double lousy. I buy cars at repossession auctions and from individuals. Most states require banks to sell the cars that they repossess at some sort of public sale. These sales are conducted many different ways, but many areas sell at public auction. The cars are often dirty, very dirty, and maybe have flat tires and dead batteries, but at the right price you can afford to buy a battery.

I purchased a Lincoln Continental worth $18,000 for $11,000 for my wife. The battery was dead and it was filthy, which scared off other bidders. After a new battery and a detailed cleanup, we had a "steal" of a car. You must have cash or certified funds to bid at most of these sales, and you need to beware of serious mechanical problems, but there are great car buys to be had.

Public Auctions

Almost anything you could wish to purchase is sold at estate sales and bankruptcy sales. Many times even brand new items are liquidated at low prices to settle estates of probate and bankruptcy. I needed a microfiche reader for my office, and after finding the price to be $400 from the dealer, I proceeded to buy a slightly used one from the classified ads for $125, after negotiating and using the "power of cash." Shortly after that, a business friend needed a reader also, but he was able to buy it for $10 at a bankruptcy auction. I guess he won that one.

When I needed to replace the copier for my offices, I began to shop my usual haunts to find a bargain. I went to a bankruptcy auction where a large law firm was being liquidated and which had ten copiers to sell. All were bringing more money than I would bid, until the last one. The best was saved for last. A copier with all the bells and whistles that sold for over $5,000 new came up for sale. The auctioneer in his haste didn't get the power cord plugged in properly and the power did not come on. Since the power didn't come on, the auctioneer said, "Well, it will make a good boat anchor." The end of the story is that I bought it for $225, had it delivered to my office, and plugged it in. It still works perfectly to this day.

Auctions are great places to get good buys; however, you have to be careful not to get caught up in the excitement of the sale and bid too much. The auctioneer's job is to hype the sale and get as much adrenaline flowing in the crowd as possible. Also, you need to understand that only "absolute" auctions sell at the price sold. If the auction is not absolute, the seller has reserved the right to reject your bid.

Garage Sales and Flea Markets

Garage sales and flea markets are also places to find good buys. Of course, you will usually have to look at a lot of junk that you do not need first. I have seen hundreds of popcorn poppers for sale, but you can get good buys on high-quality items. I go to garage sales in the affluent areas of town and find very nice items. A close friend in the financial planning business recently bought twenty custom-made $85 shirts that had been worn only once—for $1.50 each. The man selling them had gained weight and could not wear them anymore. Finding $1,700 worth of top-line dress shirts—shirts with some experience—for $30 is a good garage sale buy.

At flea markets and garage sales you should not forget to negotiate and use the power of cash. This is a good place to practice your new negotiating skills without much risk, so when the large items come along you have had some practice.

Classified Ads

The classified ads section of your newspaper is a good way to find bargains. Plus, most major cities now have papers devoted exclusively to classified ads that sell items only for individuals. Both of these should be considered excellent sources for good buys.

Not everyone wanting to sell something is a potential great buy, however; you have to look for the right ads like "must sell" or "owner desperate." If you find ads that read this way, you can call and find out the reason for selling, which should tell you just how "desperate" the owner really is. You should also find individuals here who are motivated sellers, because what you need is a great buy.

In recent years, buying on the warehouse concept through large consumer warehouses has become popular. These companies will sell to you in large volume and at purported savings, but you have to be careful. While there are many good buys in these volume purchases, some items are priced even higher than retail stores. And many times you will not use the volume required for three or four years. That is not a good bargain.

Coupons

Another way we get bargains is by clipping coupons. This seems so minor when you look at saving twenty cents, but my wife saved over $720 last year by using coupons. The warning here is not to buy what you do not need. Instead, you only use the coupons on items that you would buy anyway and look for merchants that offer "double coupon" days for extra savings. Spending just a few minutes a week and buying your food with a plan will save you many dollars.

Outlet Stores and Sales

Bargain hunting at outlet stores and at sales is the least effective method of saving, but often if you are very careful and don't forget to ask for a lower price, even these retailers will sell cheap. When a particular store is moving or has a seasonal close-out on clothing, use the cash-on-the-counter routine and ask that commissioned sales clerk how much she will cut the price if you buy several dresses. The point here is that you waited, watched, and then acted for the bargain.

Real Estate Bargains

Real estate can be a real bargain today if you watch what you are doing. For years I have bought foreclosures and have made many excellent buys. Many times I have bought houses worth $50,000 for less than $20,000. Buying foreclosures, after they have been foreclosed, from HUD or VA or the bank that foreclosed, can give you thousands of dollars in savings.

Once again, you must be extremely careful and use a good attorney who specializes in real estate if you are going to buy at actual foreclosure sales at the courthouse steps. There are many ways to get in deep trouble here, unlike what some of the tape gurus tell you. This is a very technical business, but if you buy after the foreclosure you can still get great buys without as much risk. Many times you will have to overlook some dirty carpet that needs replacing, walls that need painting, the Elvis wallpaper in the bathroom, and grass that is waist high, but for a $20,000 savings you should be able to live with that.

Owner-Financing Bonanza

Possibly the most overlooked hidden treasure is in your current home mortgage. When you bought your home, did you get owner financing? If you did, you may very well be able to save tens of thousands of dollars. As this century closes, we are seeing fewer and fewer people who have cash. And most people need cash.

If you bought your house for $120,000 with $20,000 down and the original owner carried a mortgage of $100,000 for you, you should make him a low offer for early pay-off. If he tries to sell that mortgage to raise cash, he would have trouble getting $70,000 cash for it. I recommend that you call him and make him an offer to pay him off early at $65,000 cash in the next thirty days subject to your ability to gather up the cash. (Note: This technique will not likely work if you just made the purchase.)

If he only agrees to accept $80,000 after negotiation, then you should get this agreement in writing. Next, you can arrange to refinance at $80,000 with a mortgage company. When your loan is approved and you pay him off, you have just made $20,000. However, do not use this technique to get a $100,000 loan and pocket the $20,000. Even if the mortgage company will let you, it is still not the purpose of this suggestion. The purpose is to see you free, not bind you to high payments. You have effectively bought this $120,000 house for $100,000. In a cash-poor society you will be amazed how many individual mortgage holders will deeply discount their mortgage notes for quick cash.

There are bargains everywhere if you just take time to look. Do not get the idea that only junk can be bought at a bargain. Remember, I like only good "stuff." Train yourself to search out and then negotiate for these great buys.

Waiting Is So Hard

Once you have learned basic negotiation technique and learned where to find great buys, you need to take the final and toughest step to being a big game "bargain hunter." You must learn patience. Well, here is another financial rule that requires discipline. Many times if you have the negotiation skills and have looked in the right places, but have no patience, you will still miss the bargain.

If you have sweated and strained to save, save, save—as we outlined in earlier chapters—you will have the cash. If you then get buyer's fever, and run right out and make the first or second purchase you see, you very likely will have missed the best buy.

This Was Really Fun

Years ago, when Houston, Texas, and other oil cities were having serious economic trouble, the high-priced luxury car market was deeply depressed. I decided during that time that I had to have a Jaguar automobile. I ended up buying a Jag in excellent condition with low miles, on a Monday night in the rain, for $21,000. At that time it had a retail value of $29,000. I saved $8,000! I bought it from a real estate developer who would lose it to the bank on Friday if he did not sell it that week. He was motivated and very happy to see me—and my cash.

The reason I am telling you about this purchase is that it took me six months to find the right price on the right car. I subscribed to the Houston newspaper and cut out the Jag ads every day and called every one for six months before I found the great buy I needed. You have to have patience.

What a Boss!

An administrative assistant who worked with our team years ago was renting and wanted to buy a home. Because she waited almost one year, we were able to get her and her husband, both in their twenties, a house that appraised for $134,000—for $58,300. That is a great buy, but it took patience. Believe me, that young couple had a hard time waiting that whole year, not knowing when they would find the right deal, but it appears to have been worth it.

While writing this chapter my personal car has been totaled and I am hunting for another car. I now know again that it is hard to wait and look for just that right buy. I am experiencing firsthand, again, that getting that great buy is a hassle, but my experience reminds me every morning that patience, persistence, and cash will help me "steal" a deal.

Recently I taught these concepts in a seminar. One week later a young person in his twenties called me to tell me about two possible car purchases that he had found and wanted to know which I thought he should buy. After a lengthy conversation I realized that he had the car fever really bad, which meant that patience and walking-away negotiating power were gone. I did not advise which car to buy, because those are not the only two cars in the world for sale, and neither looked to me like a particularly good buy.

Chill Out!

You have to avoid getting buying fever. When you get the fever, you lose all patience and negotiating power. You should pretend that all these purchases are a game and have some fun with it, because the retail people selling you are definitely having fun.

We must begin to think like vultures—nice vultures, to be sure, but still vultures. Now vultures are not very pretty, but the patience displayed by this animal in the wild is something we should observe. The cartoon of the two vultures on a limb, with one saying "Patience, my tail. I'm gonna kill something," may describe most of our buying habits, but we must change that to real patience.

You can have some great fun in this area of getting great buys. The more great buys you get, the more fun you will have, and the more confidence you will have in these principles. I will not tell you that these great buys are on every corner, but if you will work at negotiating, hunting buried treasure, and having patience, you will change your cash outflow dramatically. When your cash outflow is decreased, you can save even more. Then you can get even better buys. And you can save more, and so on goes the spiral of financial peace. Go for it!

Thoughts from Sharon . . .

What a bargain. If anybody loves a bargain, it is Dave and I. Fun, fun, fun.

I'm sure sometime in your life you have found a bargain. Doesn't it make you feel great? Not only are you getting a great buy, but you're saving money. What a concept.

One of the best bargains I have found is to buy consignment clothes. Yes, it was hard at first to wear used clothing, but I soon realized that washing machines and dry cleaners do a great job. Why pay retail? You can save so much buying clothes that have hardly been worn. Not only can you buy your clothes this way, but you can buy your children's too. What a deal, considering children hardly wear them out.

There's another great thing about consignment sales. You can sell your own clothes. This is a great way to have extra clothing money. Because the more money you have, the more clothes you can buy. Just look in your local newspaper during the spring and fall seasons. You'll be surprised at the sales that are listed.

Couponing is also a favorite of mine. Everyone knows how expensive grocery shopping can be, so have some fun at it. All you have to do is cut paper. It's that easy. I remember when I first started using coupons, I thought it was sort of embar-

rassing. But now, who cares? I'm saving money. After all, the more you save at the grocery, the more food you can buy.

These are just two ways I look for bargains. And every day can be a bargain day.

Peace Puppies

1. **Avoid "Stuffitis"—**The Worship of "Stuff"
2. **Plant Seeds—**Give Money Away to Worthy Causes
3. Develop Your Own **"Power over Purchase"**
4. **Find Where You Are Naturally Gifted—**Enjoy Your Work and Work Hard
5. **Live Substantially Below Your Income**
6. **Sacrifice Now** So You Can Have Peace Later
7. **You Can Always Spend More Than You Can Make**
8. **The Borrower Is the Servant to the Lender;** So Beware!
9. **Check Your Credit Report** at Least Once Every Two Years
10. **Handle Credit Report Corrections Yourself**
11. Realize That the Best Way for Delinquent Debt to Be Paid Is for You, Not Collectors, to **Control Your Financial Destiny**
12. **You Must Save Money** (the Power of Compound Interest)
13. Use the **"Keep It Simple, Stupid"** Rule of Investing
14. **Only People Who Like Dog Food Don't Save for Retirement**
15. **Always Save with Pretax Dollars—**It Is the Best Deal the Government Gives You
16. **Learn Basic Negotiating** Skills for Great Buys
17. **Learn Where to Find Great Buys** (the Treasure Hunt)
18. **You Must Have Patience** to Get Great Buys

CHAPTER FOURTEEN

Single as a One-Dollar Bill

THE FIRST THING I noticed was that she was looking down. As I watched Ramona cross the room I took note that her shoulders were stooped, she was bent forward, and she was moving painfully slowly. It didn't take a genius to realize that this lady was not a happy camper. We see Ramonas at our live events and in our Financial Peace University classes all across America. She is the single mom who has had life kicking her so hard and for so long she has lost the power to kick back. For anyone in this situation *hope* becomes a commodity they desperately need a can of. Like Popeye, she needs her spinach because Brutus has been winning too long. Fifty-two percent of the single moms in America live below the poverty level according to a study conducted by Princeton University and reported in the *Atlanta Journal-Constitution*. The question of where to go on vacation brings a sarcastic chuckle yet the idea that she could win at money again brings an instant change to her body language of defeat.

Ramona is just one type of single I want to walk with in this chapter. In general we see four types of singles:

1. Young singles, never married
2. Never married, or divorced with no kids
3. Single parents
4. Widowed after fifty

Young Singles, Never Married

Anytime you catch me using a descriptive term like this with age brackets let me give you permission to move the guidelines at will. So if the symptoms fit, you could be one of these. The young single is usually someone under thirty who is "on her own" or sort of "on his own." If I were to ask you, you would say you are carrying your own weight, but I might get a different answer from your parents. The number one problem this group has with money is *no plan*. Impulse is your byword and many of you have confused immature impulsiveness with freedom.

I am not being harsh; it is normal to wrench free from the clutches of your parents and make all your own decisions. But many young singles I have worked with over the years have pulled so hard to free themselves from childhood bondage that they stumbled when the rope was released. Part of the fun of tug-of-war is to let go when you are losing and watch the other side topple over. Parents don't do that purposely, but letting go of their kids' financial decisions can have the same effect. Newfound freedom can be confused with the right to do anything. Like a little four-year-old saying, "You are not the boss of me," some young singles seem to have no structure or limits of any kind with money.

The problem is that money is finite, and there is a limited amount of it for any of us to use. So running around impulsively buying something just because some fool bank was willing to lend you the money doesn't make it wise. Take Bobby, age twenty-four, who called my talk-radio show with money stress. He made $26,000 per year and six months before had purchased a new $22,000 car with $462 payments. What fool approved this loan? When I asked Bobby what he was thinking when he bought this car he said, "I don't know; I just wanted it."

Now before all you more mature twenty-somethings get mad at me, understand that this is one end of the spectrum and the other end is mature decisions made using wisdom. Most of you will fall somewhere in the middle. The young single can struggle because he has no rudder to guide his financial ship and, like all of us, needs a plan combined with the strength to stick to it. Much of the advice in this book simply needs to be highlighted for you in particular. First, you have to do the written plan. When you write down what you are going to do with money, you are making it and you behave. You are free to do what you want; just do it on purpose. Since you don't have the built-in accountability of a nagging spouse you have to have self-accountability, and that comes from telling yourself what to do on paper (the budget in chapter 19), then asking yourself, "Self, are you behaving in order to accomplish your goals?"

Secondly, find a money mentor. Some old rich dude. Seriously, find someone with a little gray who has proven to be wise with money. Give this person permission to hold you accountable to your budget and check with them before making large purchases. They need to love you enough to gently hurt your feelings for your own good. This person could be a parent, pastor, supervisor, or just a family friend. By the way, if you are nervous about asking someone, be aware that most high-quality people will be honored by your request. They also have the backbone to say no if they can't fully commit to the process of accountability.

Remember to budget in the fun stuff too. I'm not trying to destroy the fun you are having, but being broke because you don't have a game plan is not fun.

Thirtyplus and Never Married, or Divorced with No Kids

If you fall into this group you were smiling with all of us as we just relived our twenties. Before you grin too much, understand that your challenges are similar; you just tend to move a little more carefully because you have lived through the impulsive stage. You have wonderful freedom and have learned how that is a plus rather that a hindrance. However, you should still heed the same warnings as the younger set. While impulse isn't as big an issue, your need for a written plan to win is still there. And you still need to have a quality accountability partner to bounce large purchase decisions off of and to review your overall game plan. Your accountability partner could be a financial planner or CPA, but only if you encourage them to get personal, not just professional.

Most of the mistakes made by your group are the same mistakes we all make and that are outlined throughout this book. If I may be so bold, most of the errors we see in the never married group come from your strength to stand alone. The battles you have fought and won have made you too self-sufficient and sometimes even prideful. This overconfidence can lead to never needing anyone's help or never seeking anyone's input. Even the Lone Ranger needed Tonto. I am not saying you have to be married to be whole, but I am saying, "people need people."

In order to prosper even more in this group you need to, one, have accountability and, two, never buy what you don't understand. You found that elsewhere in this book, but just because you don't have to explain yourself doesn't mean you shouldn't be able to. Your self-reliance and independent decision making are your strength, but can be a major weakness as well.

Single Parents

This group can best be described as overworked, underpaid, tired, and many times scared out of their minds. Single parents have to do everything from chauffeuring to the attending ball games, to changing the oil. Most single parents struggle as much with time poverty as with real poverty. You run so hard and have been so close to the edge that you almost become desensitized to the fact that you could fall over that cliff.

You can be impulsive, less from immaturity than from desperation and exhaustion. You've had an unbelievably hard week, the child support didn't come, the boss wants you to work late, the day care is mad because you are late, and the tires on your car are as bald as a baby's butt. By Friday of a week like that you don't care if the ATM withdrawal of $20 fast cash for a Happy Meal causes you to bounce ten checks; you do it anyway. "You deserve a break today." I sympathize with you, but that will not let you off the hook.

You do deserve a break; the only question is, what is the best way to get a break? ATM impulsing or, worse, a credit card or, even worse, cash advance rip-offs provide momentary relief and long-term mega-pain. You are giving up the future for some quick, very temporary relief due to a personal pity party. As the famous philosopher Ursula (the sea witch in *The Little Mermaid*) says, "Life's tough, iddin it?" I'm being sarcastically mean, but you have one option as a single parent with limited money and not enough hours in a day; *plan your escape!* You are imprisoned by some circumstances you want to be free of and that takes a plan for a prison break.

The problem with prison breaks is they take a long

time—too long. Digging a hundred-yard underground tunnel over a five-year period with a spoon sounds like it takes too long and is too hard. Yet a bold plan requires a blueprint, tenacity, checking and rechecking every detail, thinking, praying, and digging every day. Sounds too tough, but on the day that you are free and the sun of liberation hits you in the face when you finally reach the end of the tunnel, you will forget. You will forget all those damp nights with the spoon and the dirt, you will forget the hopelessness you had to fight through. You will forget all the "friends" who said it couldn't be done. You will be financially free.

That happened to a friend of mine named Mary. Mary came to Financial Peace University at fifty-two years old. She came to class not to learn how to get out of debt, but to learn about investing, insurance, and real estate. I remember the night Mary looked across the room at Ramona as she told her story. Ramona was having one of "those" weeks and the tears of hopelessness were flowing. Mary told Ramona of her own years of struggle as a single mom. Heartache and setbacks seemed to be a way of life. But Mary developed a plan. She quit borrowing money. She found a mentor. She wrote down her spending *every* month *before* it happened. She vowed to wait twenty-four hours before she panicked when emergencies hit. She worked extra hours, and she took classes.

Slowly, very slowly, Mary's income rose, her power over money with "the written plan" began to work, and emergencies seemed further and further apart. Slowly, very slowly, her savings began to grow. The increased income from a career plan became investments. She refused to just exist! And Ramona smiled as Mary disclosed that on a hairdresser's income she now had more than $500,000 in mutual funds. The kids survived all this planning and even decided to live that way themselves and became prosperous adults. Mary's job became a career and later her own business; she now owns the shop.

Digging with a spoon is no fun, but if it is all you have, then *dig!* When all you have to dig with is a spoon you can't afford mistakes, so make a *plan* and stick to it. Make plans to get a shovel and later a bulldozer. If you have to take a "get by" job, do it, but take one where you can learn something and move up. Take a position where your employer will pay for your new degree, your shovel. Work everything with a five- and ten-year view; it is the only way to keep your momentum when you are digging with a spoon.

I don't think I can overemphasize that the written budget is your only way to win. Many single parents think they don't have enough money to budget, but remember: Managed money works harder. The written plan gives you power over the money you have. Money is a lion and you have to have a chair and a whip, the budget. I have watched single parents' body language change, their chins lift, their shoulders square, and even their smiles return when they get power over money. The written plan is money empowerment.

Widowed After Fifty

First, what about people who lose a spouse *before* fifty? You need to read this section *and* the section before that most pertains to you. Those of you who lose a spouse early face things similar to those of some of the folks we have discussed earlier in this chapter.

I can't imagine the pain and grief of losing your life's mate. Just the thought of losing Sharon nearly incapacitates me. To complicate the grief and loss are the financial issues that enter the scene. The hurt and emotion is blinding at a time of loss. After the death of a spouse, you must find someone who is trustworthy to help advise you on the basics. Usually, this person will not be a financial person, but more likely a family member or friend with basic financial skills. Take stock of where you are. Debts, savings, investments, life insurance, health insurance, bills, and income need to be looked at.

Once you have a good inventory you have better tools for decision making. I met with Linda, seventy-three, who had lost her husband two weeks before and was terrified. She was literally afraid she wouldn't have the money to eat, much less keep the home they had spent the last thirty years in. In just a few minutes of taking inventory of the money she had or had coming in life insurance compared to the debts, I was able to take both her hands in mine, look in her eyes, and assure her she was going to be fine. Simply absorbing that from someone she trusted about money matters made her relax instantly. Her son and I watched as she physically calmed. I don't think we realized how afraid she had been, until she no longer was. Some simple math and taking stock of what we have can soothe a hurting situation quickly.

To someone who is grieving, the big decisions bear down hard and seem to demand resolution. "Dave, I got $350,000 life insurance money. What do I do with it? I know nothing about investing and I *can't* make a mistake." "Dave, I don't think I can keep up this big house, and I'm not sure if the memories will comfort me or haunt me. Should I sell my home?" "Dave, what about paying off the mortgage?" I get hundreds of questions like these from the newly widowed about the "big stuff."

The obvious bills need to be paid, such as small debts, monthly payments, utilities, etc., but when it comes to major decisions I have an excellent suggestion. Don't. Don't make big money decisions such as selling a home, paying off a mortgage, or investing life insurance money for a while. Park the money in a six-month CD and cry. Take some time to let the edge come off the grief. If something happened to Sharon I wouldn't know what to do; I would not be in my right mind for a while. Grieving people are ripe for scams and mistakes. So a good rule of thumb is: when in doubt, don't. There will be many years of opportunity to decide about houses and mutual funds; don't rush.

Summary

Singles have the advantage of having no one to tell them what to do and no one to mess up their plan. They have the disadvantage of not having built-in accountability, so they need to get some. Get self-accountability by doing a written plan and holding yourself to it. Get outside accountability not from nosy control freaks, but from loving mentors and advisers. No impulsing allowed except that which is planned, ☺. Like the rest of us, you singles have to follow the rest of this book to win at debt reduction and wealth building; you are not the exception.

Thoughts from Sharon . . .

This is an important chapter because so many people are making the conscious decision to marry later. Some are marrying later because of careers while others just don't feel the pressure since it is normal among their set. Dave is right, though, having advisers and accountability is the only way to make good decisions and not get taken down by mistakes.

Dave and I got married at twenty-two so we have not experienced the current singles' scene except when we see the financial pain so many are in. We also have seen too many singles wed poorly because of money struggles, like the single mom who marries partly to get off poverty row. Others marry the wrong person because they completely ignore the financial warning signs that this is not a good mate.

Our hearts have always gone out to the single parents because they so often struggle with money. If you are in that category, know that you are in our prayers.

Peace Puppies

1. **Avoid "Stuffitis"**—The Worship of "Stuff"
2. **Plant Seeds**—Give Money Away to Worthy Causes
3. Develop Your Own **"Power over Purchase"**
4. **Find Where You Are Naturally Gifted**—Enjoy Your Work and Work Hard
5. **Live Substantially Below Your Income**
6. **Sacrifice Now** So You Can Have Peace Later
7. **You Can Always Spend More Than You Can Make**
8. **The Borrower Is the Servant to the Lender;** So Beware!
9. **Check Your Credit Report** at Least Once Every Two Years
10. **Handle Credit Report Corrections Yourself**
11. Realize That the Best Way for Delinquent Debt to Be Paid Is for You, Not Collectors, to **Control Your Financial Destiny**
12. **You Must Save Money** (the Power of Compound Interest)
13. Use the **"Keep It Simple, Stupid"** Rule of Investing
14. **Only People Who Like Dog Food Don't Save for Retirement**
15. **Always Save with Pretax Dollars**—It Is the Best Deal the Government Gives You
16. **Learn Basic Negotiating** Skills for Great Buys
17. **Learn Where to Find Great Buys** (the Treasure Hunt)
18. **You Must Have Patience** to Get Great Buys
19. **Singles Get Self-Accountability from the Written Plan**
20. **Singles Should Look for a Money Mentor for Advice and Accountability**
21. **Singles Beware of the Impulse Monster; He Will Eat You Alive**

CHAPTER FIFTEEN

Tying a Knot in Your Money: Marriage

MARRIAGE COUNSELORS AND STATISTICS tell us that if we can agree on four things before we marry someone, we have a much higher probability of a successful marriage, not to mention a happier, more peaceful one. The big four are; religion, in-laws, parenting, and *money*.

Larry Burkett, noted financial author, says, "Money is either the best or the worst area of communication in our marriages." After years as a financial counselor and working with marriage counselors I know that money and money fights are the number one cause of divorce, not to mention the thing we fight about the most.

Don't believe me? Well, *Worth* magazine did a detailed survey and found that the number one thing American couples fight about is money.[1] *USA Today* published the results of a study done for the Lutheran Brotherhood that shows that when we fight about money we fight most about the use of credit, shopping and spending, and then budgeting. Don't you love studies that show what we already know? *Jet* magazine published an article called "Why Money Is the Leading Cause of Divorce," which cites a study by Citibank showing that 57 percent of divorces are caused by money problems. Scripps Howard News Service is quoted in *The Detroit News* as saying that "statistics show that as many as 70 percent of divorcing couples attribute the breakdown of their marriages to arguments over money."[2]

So if you are married and have money fights, you are normal. But if this is a real problem area for you then there is also an opportunity to improve your relationship and maybe even reach agreement with your spouse. I'm not talking about agreement brought on by surrender, but rather by each one getting a vote, understanding the other's view, and finding common ground.

Let's face it, if we can agree on the checkbook there would be nothing left to fight about except who gets the remote. But there is so much to fight about, and so many opportunities to be misunderstood.

Men and Women Are Different

When it comes to money men tend to take more risks and don't save for emergencies. Men use money as a scorecard and can struggle with self-esteem when there are financial problems. Women tend to see money more as a security issue so they will gravitate toward the rainy-day fund. Because of their need for security, ladies can have a level of fear—Sharon calls it terror—when there are financial problems. Men and women are different in how they view money, and it is largely because they process problems and opportunities from different vantage points. I am speaking in generalities here, but the overall concept, though it may not apply to individuals, does apply to males and females in general. And the differences don't end with money either.

Dennis Rainey with the Family Life Marriage Seminar series tells couples that their research shows women are more verbal than men. Men usually speak about 10,000 to 20,000 words per day while women speak 30,000 to 50,000 words per day with gusts up to 125,000. That is why many men don't feel like talking after work; they have used up their quota.

In marriage expert Gary Smalley's book *Making Love Last Forever,* he lists five differences in male and female behavior that he has found through his research and years of counseling:

1. Men love to share facts; women love to express feelings.
2. Men connect by doing things; women connect by talking.
3. Men tend to compete; women tend to cooperate.
4. Men tend to be controlling; women tend to remain agreeable.
5. Men tend to be independent; women tend to be interdependent.[3]

John Gray, in his bestseller *Men Are from Mars, Women Are from Venus,* describes men as having a sense of themselves that "is defined through [their] ability to achieve results. Men are preoccupied with the 'things' that can help them express power by creating results and achieving their goals." Of women, Gray says, "A woman's sense of self is defined through her feelings and the quality of her relationships. Instead of being goal oriented, women are relationship oriented; they are more concerned with expressing their goodness, love, and caring."[4]

So What Do We Do About It?

On top of the fact that men and women are different, opposites attract. Now we have room for conflict everywhere. I discussed this and what to do about it in one of my other national bestsellers, *More Than Enough*. In that book, there is a chapter on unity, which I believe is one of the character qualities of people who win at wealth building. It is also crucial for couples dealing with their finances. Here is what I said there:

> Usually one of you is more creative and spontaneous. That mate is a little or even a lot less organized and tends to see budgeting as a form of torture or a method of the other mate controlling them. That describes Sharon. The other mate has more administrative skills and more of a bent toward numbers; there lives deep inside of this

mate a Nerd. That describes me. The Nerd can be the man or the woman and believe it or not the Nerd can be the spender or the saver. Pain has taught me to live otherwise, but my nature is the spender, while Sharon is the tightwad. Normally if one of you has all the budgeting responsibility it is the spouse with the administrative bent. The Nerd gets the budget because they are the only one that cared and they couldn't trust anyone else anyway since they are so smart. The Nerd then will do this 17 page perfect budget and present it to the family like a gloating benevolent dictator. The subjects all bow in appreciation and then go do whatever they want with the money. This unauthorized flow of money upsets the Nerd and further controls are implemented at which time the Free Spirit will dig their heels in and the budget wars are on. I have just described, maybe overstated, maybe not, how most couples "manage" money.[5]

There is a better way. Years of counseling and Financial Peace University have helped us develop a system that works. When I developed this program, I thought it was to force couples to control their spending, but one of the by-products is shared values and saved marriages. This observation about marriage is the most unexpected and thrilling discovery about this program. Here's how it works: first, the Nerd should prepare the budget, because we love to; it is our life. Instead of making the budget kingly law we should submit it to the budget committee.

The budget committee is the two of you. The budget committee has rules. Nerds, you are on my team, and Free Spirits, you are on Sharon's team. Nerds, when you submit your masterpiece budget to the committee you must remember to shut up and listen. Free Spirits will not come to any more meetings if the meeting consists of you telling them what they are going to do and how smart you are for having figured it out. By doing the first draft of the budget you have had your say. Now listen and accept the fact that your mate has valid input and agree to most of the requested changes. You are doing this to bribe them into the process of managing money, and believe me, your concessions are a small price to pay for unity.

The meeting must be short; this is a budget committee meeting, not a Camp David accord. Nerds like me love to look at all possible scenarios and do projections and pro formas. We can make Quicken a hobby. Nerds, when your objective is agreement with your Free Spirits you need to remember you have about a seventeen-minute window of opportunity before they leave. They may be physically sitting there, but their minds left and went on to non-Nerd activities that are more important to them. Nerds, your three rules for the budget committee meeting are:

1. Listen.
2. Take input.
3. Keep it brief.

Rules for the Other Side

Free Spirits, you must show up for the budget committee meeting. Yes, this activity is important to your marriage, your children's future, and the only way you can defend your position is to come to the meeting. Free Spirits, you must clean up your language. There is a phrase you can never again say. No matter what happens the rest of your life you may never again utter these words: "Whatever you want to do, Honey." Wrong, cop-out breath, you have to stick in there and make this work. And as you sit there, you must be a grown-up and realize that we cannot spend more than we make and have financial security or build wealth. Your wants, needs, and desires must be combined with your family's, and the new total must be less than your family income. Free Spirits, your three rules are:

1. Show up.
2. Give input.
3. Be realistic.

Although men and women are different and opposites attract, common sense and a success mentality tell us we have to work together. Two horses pulling a wagon can pull a huge load up a hill if they work together; pulling apart will simply turn the wagon into firewood. You need each other. The very differences that attracted you in the first place are there because you have different strengths and weaknesses. Larry Burkett says, "If two people just alike get married one of you is unnecessary."

You spenders need a saver or you will retire eating Alpo. You savers need a spender in your life, so you have a life. Working together is the only way to survive bad times and prosper in good ones. This means that when it comes to marriage, you are no longer two individuals, but one couple. Having separate bills, debts, incomes, and lives is not a marriage. The preacher said, "And now you are *one*." He didn't say, "And now you are a Joint Venture." You will never prosper like you should unless both spouses are willing to ask and answer these five questions:

1. What is our monthly income?
2. How much a month do we spend on food, gas, or kids' clothes?
3. Do we have money invested or saved anywhere?
4. Where are the wills and insurance policies?
5. What is in our retirement plans?

The Reluctant Spouse

For years I have taught that spouses must work together and one of the most consistent questions I get on our radio show and in letters is, "How do I get my spouse to join me in working on the money?" Many men are really frustrated with wives who are spoiled little girls who just want their stuff and they want it now (red-faced and lip in pouting position)! Many more women are frustrated, angry, and deeply resentful of men who refuse to help with the decision making about money. They are left shouldering the responsibility of making all the decisions and resent carrying the responsibility single-handedly. Most Nerds, whether men or women, enjoy the task of building the plan, but deeply resent being left to do all the grown-up work on their own, especially having to tolerate a spouse who persists in being a child. That sounds mean but I am seeing way too many marriages damaged by one spouse abandoning the other, financially speaking.

Getting the Reluctant Spouse Onboard

If you are having trouble getting your spouse to help with the money issues or join the get-out-of-debt crusade there are some things you don't want to do. We have all tried nagging and whining and those don't work. Don't tell them everything this book or my radio show says and how dumb they are. Beating them with an expert will only cause them to be defensive. I get e-mail often from spouses saying, "I hate you Dave, and I don't even know you. If I hear 'Dave says' one more time I'm going postal."

So what are you supposed to do? First, don't be manipulative. You and I aren't hatching a plot here. I just want to help you both get on the same page, and I want the wonderful things for your marriage that being on the same page will mean. First and foremost a little honest communication is in order. Your spouse isn't a mind reader and he may not have read this book yet. Simply explaining you are excited about getting out of debt so you can build wealth, and excited about living on a plan so you can save more, give more, and live more will excite many spouses, and they will join your newfound crusade. Tell them what you want and why. Ask them to read this book with you.

If that doesn't move you toward some good conversations then you may have to concentrate a little harder. Try writing down some of the points that concern you, explaining why. Sometimes the written word will get a spouse's attention before other things.

Men

Ladies, when you are trying to get your man's attention there are a couple of things to remember. In John Eldredge's book *Wild at Heart: Discovering the Secrets of a Man's Soul,* Eldredge says, "Deep in his heart, every man longs for a battle to fight, an adventure to live, and a beauty to rescue."[6] So when trying to get your guy to listen pose the financial situation as a battle or an adventure, or that you are a beauty that needs some rescuing. After all, all you are asking for is some help.

I often suggest, ladies, that you take both his hands in yours and press your knees against his knees and tell him that you would consider his joining your fight for financial dignity extremely romantic. Even the thickest of guys will get the hint. Gary Smalley says in his book *Making Love*

Last Forever that men respond well to two types of communication styles. One, is a rating system such as 1 to 10. It might sound like this: "Honey, on a scale of one to ten, flowers are a three and you helping me put together a plan to be debt free is a nine." Sometimes we guys hear something, but don't get how important it is to you ladies. Smalley also suggests word pictures. He has a whole book of them called *Love Languages;* I recommend it. The word picture is using a metaphor. For example: "Honey, when you blow off looking at these bills with me and I have to deal with the collectors alone, it makes me feel the same way as I would if I were kidnapped right in front of you and you did nothing to protect me." Let the emotion you are feeling—whether it's abandonment, or resentment, or whatever—show through in your word picture, but be careful not to be accusatory or use an angry tone; you don't want to put your spouse on the defensive.

Women

Men, when you are trying to get your lady onboard remember that she is wired for relationships and security. Asking any lady a question like, "How would it feel if we had $10,000 in savings just for emergencies?" will get her attention. Ninety-seven percent of women surveyed said they would like more communication in marriage. So what if you said, "Honey, I was reading about how if we spent a few minutes a week working on a budget together, it would increase our communication in every area and ultimately create more intimacy and unity. Would you like to try that?" I'm willing to bet you won't need to say much more.

Make a Sandwich

Spenser Johnson in *The One Minute Manager* suggests a pattern to use when reprimanding a subordinate. Our spouse is not our subordinate, but I have used this pattern successfully in many situations. Johnson says to create a correction sandwich. Start with honest praise of the person, then directly reprimand only the behavior you are concerned about, then close by reaffirming the person and your relationship to him. The positive on each side of the correction enables someone to swallow the reproof.

Remember we are talking about a sensitive subject here because money represents power, priorities, dreams, even fears. Jesus said, "Your treasure is where your heart is." So when you can agree on spending you have aligned your value system and will create unity. Budgeting together will create healing and communication in your marriage. If your marriage is too damaged to use these simple communication techniques to begin talking about something you have been a bit lazy about you may need to see a marriage counselor for a tune-up.

Summary

Since money problems and fights are statistically the biggest problem in marriage, any one of us who is wise will be on guard against these problems and looking for ways to win. We have heard that the Chinese symbol for danger is the same symbol used for opportunity. You have the opportunity to impact your marriage in a vastly positive way, but *you* have to do it.

Thoughts from Sharon . . .

Like most women I always want more communication. Dave, being in talk radio, is all talked out some days when he gets home and I want to talk. We have healed many of the wounds in our marriage by working on our budget together. Dave is so hard driving that for too many years I didn't speak up. I encourage you spouses who are more easygoing to hold your ground and speak your piece. After losing everything Dave took my input a lot more and now years later he has become a better listener. We don't make major decisions without each other's and God's direction. The budget committee has really helped us have a place to discuss things, and that meeting is one where Dave practices taking my input. Try it, you'll love it.

Peace Puppies

1. **Avoid "Stuffitis"—**The Worship of "Stuff"
2. **Plant Seeds—**Give Money Away to Worthy Causes
3. Develop Your Own **"Power over Purchase"**
4. **Find Where You Are Naturally Gifted—**Enjoy Your Work and Work Hard
5. **Live Substantially Below Your Income**
6. **Sacrifice Now** So You Can Have Peace Later
7. **You Can Always Spend More Than You Can Make**
8. **The Borrower Is the Servant to the Lender;** So Beware!
9. **Check Your Credit Report** at Least Once Every Two Years
10. **Handle Credit Report Corrections Yourself**
11. Realize That the Best Way for Delinquent Debt to Be Paid Is for You, Not Collectors, to **Control Your Financial Destiny**
12. **You Must Save Money** (the Power of Compound Interest)
13. Use the **"Keep It Simple, Stupid"** Rule of Investing
14. **Only People Who Like Dog Food Don't Save for Retirement**
15. **Always Save with Pretax Dollars—**It Is the Best Deal the Government Gives You
16. **Learn Basic Negotiating** Skills for Great Buys
17. **Learn Where to Find Great Buys** (the Treasure Hunt)
18. **You Must Have Patience** to Get Great Buys
19. **Singles Get Self-Accountability from the Written Plan**
20. **Singles Should Look for a Money Mentor for Advice and Accountability**
21. **Singles Beware of the Impulse Monster; He Will Eat You Alive**
22. **Men and Women View Money Differently, So Be Sensitive to Differences**

23. **Opposites Attract in Marriage, So Work Together for Maximum Wisdom**
24. **When You Agree on Spending, You Will Experience Fabulous Unity in Your Marriage**

CHAPTER SIXTEEN

Crumb Snatchers and Money

Proverbs 22:6 *"Train up a child in the way he should go and when he is old he will not depart from it."*

JACK WAS TWELVE. Jack was all boy, full of energy, and as he approached his teenage years he checked the fences, his boundaries. One day, Jack marched into the room while several other parents watched in disbelief and like a mighty general demanded money from his father. With the tilt of his arrogant little head, he announced to his dad that he was going to the movies, out for pizza, then to the mall. When his passive dad whipped out a twenty-dollar bill young Jack curled up his spiteful lip and scoffed that it wasn't enough to get across the street. As this little jerk strutted from the room with another of his compliant father's $20s (now $40 total) his dad shrugged, looked defeated, and sighed, saying, "Teenagers these days, what are you going to do?"

Jack is now twenty-four. He graduated from college

with a business degree two years ago, but works ten hours a week waiting tables. "There are no good jobs out there," he explains. He sleeps until 10:00 A.M. most mornings and goes out clubbing most nights, still using Dad's money. Mom still cleans his room and his clothes and fixes his meals. She cleans the kitchen by herself after the meal. Jack is still a jerk, only now he a large lazy jerk. His parents are at their wits' end and can't believe the choices they are faced with. "Do we move him out? Won't he starve?" "He won't pay his car payment that we cosigned for; come to think of it he isn't paying it now—we are." "He won't take responsibility, and we know this is wrong; but you can't just throw your kids in the street, can you?"

Jack is disabled. He isn't disabled in the classic sense; he just has no character, no need to win. We all know Jack, and some of you are Jack. Jack's parents caused his disability by allowing him to do nothing, and be nothing, and by giving him no instruction on how life works. Children who reach the age of eighteen with their entire skill set composed of Nintendo and eating Doritos have been abused. I am not speaking of child abuse in the sense of sexual or physical abuse, but neglect. The parents neglected the child by not giving him the character traits needed to live successfully. By giving in to every whim and attaching no consequences to actions the parents have given the child a false sense of reality. We all dislike Jack; he is lazy and has no life skills. Yet now that he is grown it is Jack's responsibility to find his way, in spite of the disability his parents have left him with.

We are raising too many Jacks in our culture. CNNFn, for example, reports that the U.S. Census Bureau says that 59 percent of men from ages eighteen to twenty-five live with their parents. Of course, there can be emergencies that occur when all of us need help from loved ones, but this is ridiculous. I disagree with the Census Bureau—59 percent are at home, but I just can't bring myself to call them "men," maybe males, but not men. If you are living at home and it is a temporary emergency, that's fine, but some of you need to get off your butts and grow a life! Before you ladies think it's just the guys, the same Census Bureau says that 48 percent of ladies from ages eighteen to twenty-five are also at home. More than half the "adult" population eighteen to twenty-five still lives with Mommy; how can that be?[1]

For starters, when the Jump Start Coalition administered a simple personal finance test to high school seniors, they averaged an F grade, correctly answering only 52 percent of the questions.[2] Is this the school's fault? Yes. Is this the parents' fault? Definitely. So what do those of us who want to parent do about teaching our kids money and life skills? Read on; I'll show you.

First, remember your children are watching you. When my oldest child was in preschool the brave (or crazy) teacher put her little feet in paint and then put the footprints on some matting. Under these precious prints she wrote, "I'm following in your footsteps." I kept that little plaque on my desk for years to remind me that they are watching. There is a Native American saying: "Tell me, and I'll forgot. Show me, and I may not remember. Involve me, and I'll understand." Our children are going to model our handling of money. The most important thing we as parents can do to teach our children is to straighten up ourselves and show them what we are doing, and why we are doing it. Jump Start says that 94 percent of children learn their money management skills from their parents.

Second, teach them intentionally. There are four main areas of money that children need to learn:

1. Work
2. Saving
3. Spending Wisely
4. Giving

Each of these areas is handled differently for different age categories. Let's look at them generally for just a moment.

Work is how money is made. There has to be an emotional and intellectual connection between work and money. I meet fifty-year-olds who have never made this connection. Because this connection needs to be made, never use the word "allowance." Instead, pay "commissions." Life will not make "allowance" for you, but it will pay you what you earn. Work, get paid; don't work, don't get paid. Work, eat; don't work, don't eat. Even the Bible says this.

Saving is how you control some of your circumstances

and how you can buy big purchases since you don't want to teach your children to borrow money. Goal setting is very important when you are saving. Try making a game out of wealth building or saving to buy something. Simply divide the price of the goal by the amount you plan to save each week to see how many weeks or months it takes to ring the bell.

Spending is done differently when you are spending money you earn. Young Jack might have had a different agenda for his evening outing had he been forced to earn that $40. Spending is also one of the rewards of disciplined saving and working; it can be the celebration of a goal reached. When spending occurs in this way the child's self-esteem is maximized, because he did it. There is a sense of accomplishment, of a job well done.

Giving is precious to watch when the kids are young, and fulfilling to watch as they grow into adulthood. Giving makes them less self-centered. Can you imagine Jack giving? I can't. Giving brings your kids depth of character. Those who never give become shallow, self-centered, and miserable adults.

Three to Six

When I was suggesting that kids work to earn commissions, some of you with small children raised an eyebrow. I am not talking about Hitler's boot camp for money. Those of us who have had little ones know the definition of cleaning the room is that we do everything except the one or two toys they actually put in the toy box, but the small child gets all the credit for cleaning the room. Give them small chores with which you assist and give them all the credit.

At this young age, pay the commission on the spot. Children need to have instant "atta boys" and money for work. This allows them to make the emotional connection and they are more willing to do the chore next time.

Likewise, the saving goals should be short. When they have saved for Celebration Barbie and they buy it, there is a sense of pride that will make you smile a lot more than if you simply bought it for them. When children are small use a clear container for the money so they can register visually the saving going up and the spending bringing their balance down.

This age typically can't do percentage systematic giving. Let their giving be spontaneous and give tons of affirmation for giving to anything. There is plenty of time later on to teach judgment about how much and where to give. Just let little Jack grab some of his cash from his jar for Children's Church; he will beam, again with the look of a job well done.

Six to Thirteen

You can judge for yourself where your child is regarding when to teach him what. Some of my kids did things with money later, some earlier. The temperament of the child will dictate when and where so the age guidelines here are up for interpretation.

We created a product called Financial Peace Junior, which is a box of teaching aids and tools for parents to work with this age group and even the younger ones. Financial Peace Junior has several very important items in it, but the core items are for teaching kids to handle money.

Since you pay your child only if he works, you need a tracking system. Try using a dry-erase board placed on the front of the refrigerator to list the chores that need to be done and how much is paid for each one. In this age bracket we suggest $5 per week for five chores: simple things like clearing away the dishes, feeding the dog, and keeping your room clean. These are things you would probably expect anyway, but paying for them gives you teachable moments about money and helps make the emotional connection between money and work. Around our house if you missed a chore one week you didn't get paid for it; if you missed it for too long your life was in danger. Some chores should be done with no pay just because you are part of the family, but if they are all done that way there are no teachable money moments. Little Jack doesn't "feel the pain" of a movie ticket if the sweat of his brow isn't associated with the money.

Once the work is done have a payday. At this age, payday should be once a week. Financial Peace Junior has three envelopes in it to divide the money earned between spending, saving, and giving. Spending and giving at this age fosters problem-solving skills as the goal setting can get really detailed, depending on the particular child.

In our family, saving started to get serious at this age because we announced to our children that we would not be buying cars for our teenagers nor would we allow them to buy a car on credit. My first child started saving for her car when she was ten. By the time she was fourteen she had picked out the kind of car she wanted and was looking at prices. Since we have been blessed financially, we have instituted 401DAVE for their cars, matching their savings dollar for dollar. Our first daughter saved $4,500 and we matched that amount. She and I shopped for months until we bought a really nice Mustang at below wholesale book for $9,000 cash. The two younger children saw no leeway in the formula, saw we weren't kidding, so they poured on the work and even started looking for ways to make money outside the family. We don't pay for insurance or tires either. If teens pay their own insurance they tend to know what the speed limit is and actually stop at stop signs. When teens buy their own tires they don't turn them over more than is needed to roll the car forward. I personally think it is brain damage to buy a sixteen-year-old a brand new car with everything paid for. Where are they going to get that deal out in the real world? All that does is teach my daughters to look for a Sugar Daddy instead of a committed relationship where both husband and wife are responsible and share goals. It is teaching my son that somewhere out in the real world there is some magic fairy dust that coughs up cars. The only magic fairy dust I've found is cash.

Fourteen to Outta Here

Fourteen-year-olds are emotionally four one day and thirty the next. Teenagers are very fun to mess with and teach because they are trying so hard to be adults and be cool at the same time. Treat your children as adult as they are acting. Our kids, for example, were ready to handle an entire household budget by their teenage years because we had intentionally walked them to that point during the other two phases.

At fourteen, if you have them ready and their temperament is correct, release their own budgets to them. We opened a checking account for them with a debit card, but remember: *no credit cards!* We then established what portion of our budget was going to their clothes, entertainment, etc. Then we explained to them that from now on we were no longer paying for virtually anything directly, but we would be giving them X dollars per month to live on. If our daughter buys one dress and blows it all, she can't go to the movies. If our son eats at expensive restaurants with his friends, no new clothes for school. It was very rewarding to watch the lessons that we had been teaching them over many years go into overdrive. The bargain shopping, the conscious decision making, and the discipline were extreme, adultlike, and gratifying. The giving was systematic, God led, and mature. Teenagers will feel very adult and act like it, and you will have the feeling that all your years of training are paying off. Your teen will learn to balance her checkbook every month. You will watch your child decide how to spend his money rather than blow it all without thought. Don't get me wrong, you will have your trying times, but your kids will have a sense of power over money while many of their friends will be functioning financially at a four-year-old level.

You will have the normal power struggles over who is in charge, especially since you do not give up your veto power just because your children make or manage their money. They may feel more empowered and that may even aggravate some of the power struggles, but I would rather your kids and mine have the sense of power than be a helpless, hapless twenty-four-year-old Jack. In other words, you still decide which bathing suits are too revealing, what hair color will work, and whether or not they get their tongues pierced, even if you pay for it. By empowering the teen with money management you do not abdicate your right or responsibility to parent.

Summary

I can think of nothing Sharon and I have done with our lives that is as fulfilling and rewarding as raising our children. They are not perfect, and we are not perfect; but we are very proud of what they have become and are becoming. You are teaching your children how to live life well when you build their character and money management skills. Teach your children how to handle money or they will come home and live with you forever.

Thoughts from Sharon . . .

Growing up on the farm, we were taught hard work early in life. Later my parents owned a local convenience store and we worked there afternoons and summers. Dave also grew up with a strong work ethic so it has been natural for us to demand that working hard becomes a character quality our kids have.

A mother's heart wants them to be kids, but Mom also needs the help in the kitchen and around the house. It was especially fun for me when our kids were little as they learned to do a chore and got the pay. Their little chests would stick out with pride as they said, "Mommy, come look at my clean room." The giving heart of children just melts my heart sometimes. As a mommy I have been the nurturer and sometimes the tough guy, but my kids have been the most rewarding experience of my life.

Peace Puppies

1. **Avoid "Stuffitis"—**The Worship of "Stuff"
2. **Plant Seeds—**Give Money Away to Worthy Causes
3. Develop Your Own **"Power over Purchase"**
4. **Find Where You Are Naturally Gifted—**Enjoy Your Work and Work Hard
5. **Live Substantially Below Your Income**
6. **Sacrifice Now** So You Can Have Peace Later
7. **You Can Always Spend More Than You Can Make**
8. **The Borrower Is the Servant to the Lender;** So Beware!
9. **Check Your Credit Report** at Least Once Every Two Years
10. **Handle Credit Report Corrections Yourself**
11. Realize That the Best Way for Delinquent Debt to Be Paid Is for You, Not Collectors, to **Control Your Financial Destiny**
12. **You Must Save Money** (the Power of Compound Interest)
13. Use the **"Keep It Simple, Stupid"** Rule of Investing
14. **Only People Who Like Dog Food Don't Save for Retirement**
15. **Always Save with Pretax Dollars—**It Is the Best Deal the Government Gives You
16. **Learn Basic Negotiating** Skills for Great Buys
17. **Learn Where to Find Great Buys** (the Treasure Hunt)
18. **You Must Have Patience** to Get Great Buys
19. **Singles Get Self-Accountability from the Written Plan**
20. **Singles Should Look for a Money Mentor for Advice and Accountability**
21. **Singles Beware of the Impulse Monster; He Will Eat You Alive**
22. **Men and Women View Money Differently, So Be Sensitive to Differences**

23. Opposites Attract in Marriage, So Work Together for Maximum Wisdom
24. When You Agree on Spending, You Will Experience Fabulous Unity in Your Marriage
25. Teach Children to Work, Spend Wisely, Save, and Give
26. The Most Powerful Legacy You Can Leave Is Wise, Competent Children

CHAPTER SEVENTEEN

Family, Friends, and Money

THE NUMBER OF OUR relationships with family and friends that are strained over money is unbelievable. How many grown brothers and sisters don't speak over a bad loan, jealousy on an inherited item, or worse yet, appropriately denied help? Friendships and extended family relationships are often strained to the max or even broken because of some kind of money issue.

I often get calls on my radio show like the one I recently received from Bob, a distraught father. Bob's daughter, age twenty-one, and son-in-law, twenty-four, the parents of his only grandchild, had taped an envelope to his door. The note said they were to be evicted the next day if they didn't come up with $1,500 in back rent. Why taped to the door? Shame. Six months earlier Bob had already caught up the rent once. When Bob called his son-in-law's parents, he learned that the young man's mom, who co-signed for a $10,000 finance company loan, was paying the monthly payments and had been for six months. This was the loan that was going to get them over the hump, make everything OK. His mom had also recently caught up the electric bill before it was disconnected. I asked if the young people were ill or having a job crisis, and Bob informed me they both had jobs and seemed to earn "good money." These two sets of loving parents/grandparents were being milked.

Ann also called my show that same week scared and confused. Her mother, seventy-two, had been widowed three years earlier. Her mom had never handled money while Dad had always made everything work out. Mom had pretty well gotten whatever she wanted throughout her married life. Dad left her a paid for $140,000 house, $30,000 cash, and no life insurance. Mom had spent her way through the cash plus another $35,000 in credit card debt. So Ann's mom is now seventy-two, broke, with a debt-free house and $900 per month in Social Insecurity. Mom had called demanding that Ann and her husband pay off the credit cards because "that is what a good daughter would do." When Ann asked about some of the specifics of the financial situation she was verbally slapped down for interfering.

The friend at work who needs $50 until Friday, the brother who wants to open a "no miss" business but needs $20,000 of your money, or the grown child who can't seem to find himself all make us question our sanity. Are we mean, tight, or greedy if we don't cave in? Are we weak, spineless, or a sucker if we do help out? The answer to all these questions is complicated and yet simple. A proper perspective and some sound financial principles by which to lead your life will give you the answers when you face tough decisions.

If you are facing one of the situations I have outlined, I suggest you buy a fabulous book called *Boundaries* by Dr. Henry Cloud and Dr. John Townsend. Dr. Cloud has been a guest on my radio show and I have heard him speak numerous times; his material will be food for your soul. These problems are not money problems but rather relationship problems involving boundaries. Dr. Cloud describes boundaries this way: "Just as homeowners set physical property lines around their land, we need to set mental, physical, emotional, [I'll add financial] and spiritual boundaries for our lives to help us distinguish what is our responsibility and what isn't."[1]

When someone wants something of mine, whether it is my time, my money, or my influence, I look carefully at the request. If I comply am I truly helping them or am I giving a drunk a drink? If I fulfill the request am I true to my beliefs? For instance, I am a Christian, so it would be inconsistent for me to give money to build a house of worship for another faith. I don't believe in debt, co-signing, or living without a plan, so it would be inconsistent for me to co-sign a loan to pay off debts while the mismanagement continues. I would just be giving a drunk a drink and end up paying that loan. I have carefully outlined financial principles in this book that I really live, so to ask me to advertise on my radio show for a car dealer telling you to lease your car is a waste of time; I won't. I don't have to be mean about setting these boundaries, but I must be firm or I must not really believe the financial principles I'm trying to get you to practice. I'm not selfish, greedy, uncaring, or hurtful because I have principles that tell me I must deny your request for help. I will try to help you another way that is more helpful to you and consistent with my life standards.

The problem is immature manipulative people can interpret your "no" to their request as mean or uncaring, when the reality is the "no" is based on the fact that you do care. We are not bound by friendship or blood to participate in an irresponsible adult's fantasy about how life really works. Dr. Cloud says this: "Many adult children perpetually get into financial messes because of irresponsibility, drug or alcohol use, out-of-control spending, or the modern 'I haven't found my niche' syndrome. Their parents continue to finance this road of failure and irresponsibility, thinking that 'this time they'll do better.' In reality, they are crippling their children for life, preventing them from achieving independence. An adult who does not stand on his own financially is still a child. To be an adult, you must live within your means and pay for your own failures." So when you help someone in a way that reinforces his stupid behavior rather than causes him to grow away from it you are codependent. Cloud says, "Codependents are not doing good; they are allowing evil because they are afraid."

So Bob and his in-laws were afraid to not pay the back rent and co-sign loans even though they knew it wasn't going to help as long as there was continued irresponsibility, overspending, and mismanagement. They were afraid the grandbaby would be homeless or hungry so their grown kids were holding them hostage. I told Bob to do three things. One, get on the phone to the in-laws and get them on the same page with him. Two, give no more money unless the grown kids are willing to go to Financial Peace University (for which I donated the tuition conditionally) and submit a written monthly budget to both sets of parents for six months. Three, if they didn't like this tell them no more money! Also, tell them if the grandbaby is hungry or homeless let him know and Bob or the in-laws would buy food (but not give the parents cash), and let the baby stay with them until these "grown-ups" figure out how to live.

If that sounds harsh to you I'll tell you it isn't; it is very tough, but not harsh. Harsh is to allow these "grown-ups" to continue to live in denial about their habits. They asked for help and Bob is not required to answer their request in any way he feels uncomfortable with. If you ask for my money or my help I am obligated to give it in the way I think is most helpful, and if you don't like that then you don't have to take my help.

For Ann's situation, I suggested that if she wanted to help it would be on the condition that Mom would cut up all the credit cards, agree to live on a $900 per month written budget, and would be accountable to Ann for that behavior change. Ann's response was that Mom would be outraged at the intrusion. Maybe so, but hasn't Mom just called and asked Ann for $35,000? OK. Sometimes when you set boundaries it makes manipulators angry. Ann will have to live with that if she respects herself, her husband, and her children. Sometimes people feel guilty for not caving. That is normal, but remember in both cases we offered to *give* money, only with guidelines that blessed the receiver of the gift. So what's to feel guilty about?

When you do help friends and family, I recommend you never borrow money for them or loan them money. Remember, the borrower is a slave to the lender and you will drive a wedge into the relationship. The old joke is, "If you loan your brother-in-law $100 and he never speaks to you again was it worth it?" If you don't have the cash to help, you aren't in a position to help and your honest answer should be you don't have the money.

The Other Kind

What do you do with friends and relatives who are messing up their financial lives and don't ask for help? Technically it is none of your business, but we all hate to watch people we love doing stupid things that are wrecking their lives. Don't answer questions that weren't asked, so if someone you love is goofing up you have to get them to ask for help. If they are not open to input then you are intruding into a place you aren't welcome, and you should just love and pray for them. Parents who continually interfere in the financial lives of their kids without permission are jerks; they haven't the maturity to let their kids grow up. Grown kids who interfere in their parents' lives without permission are disrespectful and out of line. It is hard to watch people misuse their lives when we love them, so get them to ask for your help. But if you can't get their permission you are meddling and as my grandmother used to say, "Those convinced against their will are of the same opinion still."

I have found a few ways to get people to ask for my help. One simple one is to go to them and say, "If you ever see me doing something stupid I want you to know that we are close enough that I would expect you to tell me." Usually the loved one will say, "Ditto." Boom, you just got permission. "Well now that you mention it . . ." Another way I use is to tell of my failures and shortcomings and then say what I learned from it (the lesson they need to learn) and how prosperous I am now that I have applied those lessons. In a one-on-one conversation that often will open the dialogue and the loved one will ask about what they should do. By admitting your failures you give them permission to have struggles too. We have all failed and we should use that to help the people we love by being real. Another thing I do is talk about this or that great book I just read that really helped me, and they might want to read it to see if there is someone they know who needs the help. This is particularly effective when you can't get your loved one to ask you about the subject. If you decide to give a book such as *Financial Peace* to someone, write a note explaining how you once messed up and this material helped you; otherwise you may insult your loved one rather than help!

Warnings

When parents are dealing with grown children be sure to get permission to do anything with money whether it is a large gift or advice. If you don't get permission first the gift of money or wisdom can easily be taken as interference and probably is. A good friend of mine went broke several years ago and his mother-in-law gave him and his family $50,000 cash two years later without a word of explanation. My friend took this as an insult to his ability to provide for his family. I told him if the money was giving him that much trouble he could send it to me. As it turns out I know his mother-in-law well and she meant nothing except good things by the gift; she had sold a part of the family farm and was dispersing the proceeds to be nice. A simple note or phone call from her could have made the gift a blessing rather than an insult.

Dan called my radio show recently saying his wife's parents were continually giving big monetary gifts unsolicited and were attaching strings to them. One of the strings was that his wife was to put the money in her name only and not tell him where she invested it. I told him he was nicer than me because there would have been a showdown at the OK corral if that happened at my house. He mentioned that his marriage grew weaker every time they did this. I told him his wife was going to make a choice someday between her marriage and her parents' obvious ploy and interference. My advice to him was to seek marriage counseling and to ask his wife to go with him so the counselor could help her with healthy boundaries.

When children are trying to advise or help parents with monetary gifts it can get real sticky. I once heard the problem here called "the powdered butt syndrome." Once someone has powdered your butt they have trouble taking advice about money or sex from you. As the baby boom generation's parents age we are facing real problems with parents' financial misbehavior. Balancing boundaries and obligation can be very difficult. I am bound to honor my parents. That means to help them as much as I can in ways that are consistent with my beliefs and principles. In other words if Ann's mom had not asked for help and lost her home, Ann might feel that paying for food and shelter was what she wanted to do. Or she might offer to let Mom move in with her as long as everyone agreed in advance on the terms of this arrangement. It is not spiritually or mentally healthy to allow guilt to force us to provide help that violates these boundaries.

A Note to Boomers

I am finding, as are many other financial professionals, that the largest financial expense boomers may be facing is not their kid's college, but their parents' nursing home or in-home care. Long-term care insurance (nursing home and in-home care insurance) is a necessity for anyone over sixty. If your parents don't have long-term care insurance and can't afford it, buy it for them if you can. Talk to your parents about wills and insurance if your relationship allows for this kind of conversation. It could save your family hundreds of thousands of dollars in health care and taxes.

Summary

Get yourself in great financial condition; get rich so you can help the ones you love. Make sure as you are helping that you are not enabling stupid behavior to continue. Also, make sure you are helping and not interfering.

Thoughts from Sharon . . .

I don't tend to have much mercy for able-bodied adults, it is the kids in these loved ones' families that tug at my heart. We have had friends whose siblings and parents continually nag them for money and never take advice, I have little patience for that.

I will go beyond what Dave might do where a child is concerned. The little children shouldn't suffer for their parents' mistakes, but so many do. Because of what we do in teaching money, many of our friends and a few of our relatives have asked advice, sometimes taking it. It is most gratifying when our loved ones are inspired to follow our example and are able to win with money.

Peace Puppies

1. **Avoid "Stuffitis"—**The Worship of "Stuff"
2. **Plant Seeds—**Give Money Away to Worthy Causes
3. Develop Your Own **"Power over Purchase"**
4. **Find Where You Are Naturally Gifted—**Enjoy Your Work and Work Hard
5. **Live Substantially Below Your Income**
6. **Sacrifice Now** So You Can Have Peace Later
7. **You Can Always Spend More Than You Can Make**
8. **The Borrower Is the Servant to the Lender;** So Beware!
9. **Check Your Credit Report** at Least Once Every Two Years
10. **Handle Credit Report Corrections Yourself**
11. Realize That the Best Way for Delinquent Debt to Be Paid Is for You, Not Collectors, to **Control Your Financial Destiny**
12. **You Must Save Money** (the Power of Compound Interest)
13. Use the **"Keep It Simple, Stupid"** Rule of Investing
14. **Only People Who Like Dog Food Don't Save for Retirement**
15. **Always Save with Pretax Dollars—**It Is the Best Deal the Government Gives You
16. **Learn Basic Negotiating** Skills for Great Buys
17. **Learn Where to Find Great Buys** (the Treasure Hunt)
18. **You Must Have Patience** to Get Great Buys
19. **Singles Get Self-Accountability from the Written Plan**
20. **Singles Should Look for a Money Mentor for Advice and Accountability**
21. **Singles Beware of the Impulse Monster; He Will Eat You Alive**
22. **Men and Women View Money Differently, So Be Sensitive to Differences**

23. Opposites Attract in Marriage, So Work Together for Maximum Wisdom
24. When You Agree on Spending, You Will Experience Fabulous Unity in Your Marriage
25. Teach Children to Work, Spend Wisely, Save, and Give
26. The Most Powerful Legacy You Can Leave Is Wise, Competent Children
27. Giving Loved Ones All the Money They Request May Not Be Best for Them
28. Making Decisions Based on Fear of Reprisal Can Be a Sign of Codependence
29. Be Strong Enough to Help Others and Strong Enough Not To

CHAPTER EIGHTEEN

Carefully Consider Counsel

IT IS TIME for all of us to grow up enough to quit thinking that we are the "John Wayne" of our finances. You do not have the corner on all the knowledge of the financial world, nor do I. You cannot ride in on your white horse, make snap decisions, implement quickie strategies, and still be ready for the next commercial. Our financial lives are more complex in this time than the consumer or even the professional investor can fully comprehend on his own. The man, woman, or couple who makes significant financial decisions without careful consideration of outside counsel first is destined for pain and heartache.

Home Is Where the Heart Is

The very first place counsel should be sought is in your home. Yes, your spouse does have a brain and one that may even work better than yours. The traditional sexist relationship where the wife is not involved in matters of money is not only shortsighted, it is also just plain dumb. On the other hand, the "modern" woman who allows her husband to completely dump all the finances on her is not only being mistreated, she is also missing out on basic opportunities of communication in a good marriage. Do you think these are strong statements? Well, how is it supposed to be? I normally see that one of the two partners is naturally more adept at handling numbers and keeping up with budgets, and I believe that person should do so. It doesn't matter whether this person is the man or the woman. That person should keep the records, but that person should not make all the decisions.

We Gotta Talk

As you might have guessed, in my home I am the one who likes numbers, but before I write the monthly bills or make a purchase of significance, I have learned to review a summary with my wife. This review forces me to look carefully at priorities, because I have to show her what these priorities are. More importantly, however, it gives us a point of clear communication on where we are and where we are going, so there are no surprises later.

You would be amazed at the number of men who have been in my office who hated to keep the checkbook, but who thought it was their duty to do so as head of the household. The result was inefficient recordkeeping and management by someone operating outside his natural gifts. Such a man, who turns the recordkeeping over to his gifted wife and yet does not surrender all the decision making, is wise and has lost no footing.

But sometimes we carry ideas too far. I have seen couples who figured out that in their particular marriage the wife was the "numbers" person; then not only were the recordkeeping duties given to her, but all of the financial decisions as well. Any time one member of a marriage is making most or all of the financial decisions without the consultation of the other, the basic communication of the marriage is lacking, and this couple is usually headed for financial problems. It is just common sense: two heads are better than one.

It Is Common Sense

Money has such a dynamic that it plays a role in our relationships many times, even when we don't realize it. You might say, "I am not controlled by money." You may be one of those people for whom money has very little impact, but to assume that it does not play a significant role in your relationships and even in your marriage is naive. You will benefit if you learn to communicate with your spouse and take counsel from him or her. I know it is time-consuming and even humbling to openly discuss money at home. If you don't, however, you will have some difficult lessons ahead.

One more note to men: If you do not draw on all your resources when making decisions, you are not wise. Many men in this country still have a "macho" need to completely control all financial matters, and many wives even like it this way. That's the wrong move. Guys, God gave women a sixth sense called women's intuition, which He did not give us. Most women have the ability to come to the right decision even if they totally misunderstand or have not a clue about the data. I am a very logical person so I fought this for years—and I can't tell you how much money it cost me and how much I've saved since taking my wife's advice. Women often get the right answer by "feeling" it.

The World's Greatest Financier

Several years ago I found an investment house to buy to fix up for resale and profit. The foundation had collapsed and the house needed major repairs. After carefully figuring my repair costs, including getting bids on the work to be done, I bought the house for $6,200. At that great price, plus the work to be done, I determined that my profit would be over $30,000 on this one deal. I was excited. I had made the deal of deals! Since my wife has a college degree in a totally separate area than finance and hates numbers and dealing with money matters, I never used to bother her with my deals. I just brought home the bacon.

I took this sweet woman out to see my "deal," which of course looked awful because work was just beginning. When we drove up in front of the house she immediately said that I had gotten a bad deal, that she just felt it. So for the entire thirty-minute ride home, I preached to her about her lack of ability to see past the work to be done and about her lack of ability with the basics of business and finance.

Soon the repairs to the house and the foundation were completed at the predicted price estimates, and I was ready for big profits. One day as we were trying to sell that property, I drove up in front and to my horror my new foundation had fallen. We put up another wall, and it fell too. As we replaced the foundation the third time we discovered a wet weather spring running against the front of the home. We were able to redirect the spring, and the foundation stands today, but I ended up losing over $25,000 on my great "deal." So I repeat the point: never underestimate the power of your spouse's counsel. (P.S. She never said, "I told you so," but I deserved it.)

The Big Spender

One more stereotype on the subject of marriage and money also should be dispelled here. Larry Burkett in his money management teachings talks about this phenomenon, and I must concur. In my experience counseling couples through troubled financial situations, I have not found women to have the overspending problem. When a woman goes crazy spending, she usually redecorates a room or buys some clothes, and the dent is $500 to

$1,500. But when a man goes crazy, he comes home with an elaborate investment of $50,000 in a new llama breeding technique or buys a third car (his toy on which, of course, he thinks he can make a profit) for $15,000. Not all, but most women tend to be the ones who watch the household finances with a conservative eye. I think this comes from a maternal instinct to protect the home.

Good Ole Mom & Dad

We should also consider counsel from our parents. In our teenage years we struggle and finally wrench free from what we perceive as bondage to our parents. Now we are free at last to make our own decisions. Many of us have made such a giant leap into our so-called adulthood that even many years later we have trouble coming back to our parents for advice.

Those of us who have not utilized this source of wise counsel have missed many an opportunity to avoid pain, as well as the opportunity to develop rich adult-to-adult relationships with our parents. It takes an emotionally secure person to seek and seriously consider the counsel of parents. Too often we hear disrespectful, angry statements like "old fool." Let me assure you, there are very few *old* fools, because living their lives watching young fools has made them wise.

> **Proverbs 12:15** *"The way of a fool is right in his own eyes, but he who hears counsel is wise."*

Your Pastor

You should also seek counsel from your spiritual leader, that is, your pastor, priest, or whatever title given to the person who guides and instructs you in spiritual and eternal matters. If you are willing to trust your eternal soul to this person's direction, you should also seek his or her counsel in financial matters. As a Christian I believe God will give my pastor wisdom in matters he might not seem to have access to through his background or education. So I will seek his advice in decisions of importance.

Along the same spiritual lines, my primary counsel is the counsel of God through prayer.

The Experts

Lastly, you should seek out the opinions and viewpoints of the "experts." You can seek their knowledge through personal discussions and/or by reading the many books or publications available on a given subject. But you should be careful *not* to take advice solely from an expert who makes a sales commission when you follow his "advice." Many well-informed and well-meaning brokers are more than willing to give you their "expert" counsel, but there is an inherent conflict of interest in the way they get paid. Many times the integrity is sterling and the advice proper; sadly, just as many times it is not.

If your "financial planner" wants you to invest in a Hybrid African Beetle Tax Shelter, but your wife and parents think it is not smart, you might take more time to consider the matter. You should avoid getting caught in the "they-don't-understand-intricate-financial-transactions" syndrome, because Mother may really know best.

Striking a Balance

The balance of considering and weighing counsel from various sources to come to the proper decision is not an easy task. I have found that weighing the counsel is not the usual problem for people, but rather that they did not take time to seek *any* counsel at all. We move too fast. We get "buying fever" and don't want anyone to tell us not to do it—until after the crash. Then we want to know why no one told us not to make that purchase. We have to make ourselves slow down and seek the counsel of love, experience, and knowledge before making significant financial moves.

Thoughts from Sharon . . .

In order to become wiser, we should learn to seek advice from others. Yes, sometimes this is hard to do. It starts when we learn to build faith and trust in others.

Communicating with those closest to you is important. A lot of times this will be your spouse or best friend. By giving all the facts about the situation, the two of you can gather the information more wisely.

Have you ever gone to a new city on a vacation or business trip? During this trip have you picked up a city map? Maps give answers to questions such as which interstate to take or what direction to head. Maps also give us insight and knowledge about strange cities.

Years ago, Dave and I were on vacation. What a great time we had sightseeing—until we became lost. As we passed several gas stations, I begged my husband to pull over and ask for help. "No, I know where I am going," he responded. So he thought.

Well, thirteen miles later we stopped. He had gotten us off course. If he had listened to my advice, we would have been eating a lot earlier than we did.

Your spouse just may know what he or she is talking about. Why not listen?

Peace Puppies

1. **Avoid "Stuffitis"—**The Worship of "Stuff"
2. **Plant Seeds—**Give Money Away to Worthy Causes
3. Develop Your Own **"Power over Purchase"**
4. **Find Where You Are Naturally Gifted—**Enjoy Your Work and Work Hard
5. **Live Substantially Below Your Income**
6. **Sacrifice Now** So You Can Have Peace Later
7. **You Can Always Spend More Than You Can Make**
8. **The Borrower Is the Servant to the Lender;** So Beware!
9. **Check Your Credit Report** at Least Once Every Two Years
10. **Handle Credit Report Corrections Yourself**
11. Realize That the Best Way for Delinquent Debt to Be Paid Is for You, Not Collectors, to **Control Your Financial Destiny**
12. **You Must Save Money** (the Power of Compound Interest)
13. Use the **"Keep It Simple, Stupid"** Rule of Investing
14. **Only People Who Like Dog Food Don't Save for Retirement**
15. **Always Save with Pretax Dollars—**It Is the Best Deal the Government Gives You
16. **Learn Basic Negotiating** Skills for Great Buys
17. **Learn Where to Find Great Buys** (the Treasure Hunt)
18. **You Must Have Patience** to Get Great Buys
19. **Singles Get Self-Accountability from the Written Plan**
20. **Singles Should Look for a Money Mentor for Advice and Accountability**
21. **Singles Beware of the Impulse Monster; He Will Eat You Alive**
22. **Men and Women View Money Differently, So Be Sensitive to Differences**
23. **Opposites Attract in Marriage, So Work Together for Maximum Wisdom**

24. **When You Agree on Spending, You Will Experience Fabulous Unity in Your Marriage**
25. **Teach Children to Work, Spend Wisely, Save, and Give**
26. **The Most Powerful Legacy You Can Leave Is Wise, Competent Children**
27. **Giving Loved Ones All the Money They Request May Not Be Best for Them**
28. **Making Decisions Based on Fear of Reprisal Can Be a Sign of Codependence**
29. **Be Strong Enough to Help Others and Strong Enough Not To**
30. **Listen to Your Spouse's Counsel** (Women's Intuition)
31. There Are Few "Old" Fools—**Seek Experienced Counsel**

CHAPTER NINETEEN

Why Written?

WHAT WOULD YOU SAY the chances of success are for a business that keeps no records and does no forecasting of income or expenses? I would say the chances for failure are very high, and the chances of success are slim to none. The Small Business Administration says that the number-one reason for small business failure is poor recordkeeping.

Is Your Business Going Broke?

This fact comes as no surprise to most of us, and 90 to 95 percent of American households operate without a detailed accurate written outline of income and expenses. They have only a slight clue as to what it takes to keep their household "in business" every month. Not one in 150 people that I have counseled for financial woes had an accurate list of obligations and expenses when they first come to me. No one does it! To use some overworked expressions: When we fail to plan, we plan to fail, and so there is always too much month left at the end of the money.

More Dirty Words

I have bad news. Everyone needs a written budget. When I say this I hear things like, "A budget, oh no, not me! I am a free spirit!" or "No budget for me—things are pretty well under control" or "Only nerds do written budgets. You know, the guys with the calculators on their belts who don't have anything better to do on Saturday night." Wrong, wrong, wrong.

The word "budget" is a derivative of the French word *bougette*, a form of *bouge*, which is a small leather purse. When we discuss budgets we think of small amounts, of stinginess, of a dark room where we can't get out. With these perceptions it is no wonder we don't plan our cash flow on a monthly basis.

We view budgeting as if it is a form of torture. A correctly prepared budget is not a form of torture, nor is it so time consuming that you can't have Saturday night out. On the contrary, a proper, simple, written plan will actually give you more free time and money with which to enjoy it.

The Amazing Growing Money

I counseled a young single man recently about putting some simple budgeting measures and plans in place. He soon called to say it was as if his money had grown, as if money was coming in from nowhere. Okay, if you don't want to call it a budget call it a "cash flow plan," maybe that won't seem so harsh. But we must implement some written strategies for forecasting and controlling our money.

Developing a budget or cash flow plan doesn't sound like much fun, does it? Does going to Europe, to Cancun to scuba dive, or to Aspen to snow ski—and coming home to face no debt or credit card bills sound like fun? That is what a proper plan will do for you because you can begin planning that debt-free vacation as a part of your plan today. If you are a free spirit and want to have more freedom or time to write or paint, then you can plan financially to attain that status. But until you plan, you will never reach "free spirit" status financially because "unexpected" bills will always clip your wings.

It Is Not a Whip

A cash flow plan is not a method of manipulation for one family member over another. I know in some households the term is used in such a negative connotation that most people would rather have termites in the house than a written budget. But you have to realize that that approach is a misuse of the idea. It is the reflection of the character of the manipulator, not of the concept of cash flow control.

A good written plan comes from the communication

and input of all family members and is implemented by the joint efforts of all family members. I keep saying simple plan, because a good plan should not be time consuming. Most experts agree that an accurate plan can first be developed in two to six hours and should be able to be maintained in less than fifteen minutes a week. If you are spending more time than that on the average household budget, you are leaving things out and thereby putting stress on the plan, or you have overcomplicated it. You should kiss your budget too—keep it simple, stupid.

I Said, "Written"

Sometimes I hear, "Well, I kinda sorta know where my money is, ya know. I know what it is going to, ya know. I do my planning in my mind, ya know." Having a *written* plan is absolutely necessary. Have you ever had a problem that you thought you needed the input of someone else to answer? And when you began to tell that person the whole situation you were able to answer the question for yourself? You found yourself answering your own question, leaving the other person wondering why you asked.

This happens to us for a reason. The scattered information in your brain has to be categorized, summarized, and organized very quickly to verbalize it. This clarification of information, which has occurred for the sake of communication, clears your mind and allows you to answer your own question. Then we say something like, "I just needed to bounce it off someone."

The Clearing of a Fog

Developing a written plan does the exact same thing for your finances. To accurately develop a plan you have to gather, organize, categorize, and analyze information about your money situation. We will *never* do this unless we put our situation on paper. As you begin to organize this information, you will be amazed that answers to problems will appear easily.

The accurate picture is just the first benefit, however. Something mystical happens when we commit something personal to writing. We somehow begin to live out our plans. I am not saying that if you do a written plan you will fall into a trance and automatically carry out the very last detail. Clarifying your goals and aspirations, and then facing financial realities, changes the way you see your situation. When you see what must be done, you will begin to move in that direction as a matter of course. Honestly, the *only* way most of you will ever see that exotic vacation, one that you probably deserve, is to have a written plan that controls household income and expenses to enable you to begin saving for it.

Are you wondering how to get to this magical place known as "cash flow plan land"? I promise not to leave you here with just vague suggestions. I will present three specific steps you can follow to develop a written cash flow plan. Easy-to-follow instructions and forms are in the appendix to help you develop your written plan.

It is as easy as A - B - C.

STEP A:
Keep Your Checkbook Properly Recorded and Balanced

Sounds so simple, doesn't it? Then why do so few people do it? Bank officers tell horror stories of people who bring in checking accounts so far out of balance the only thing that can be done is close them out and start over with a new account. The math involved in keeping and balancing a checkbook is basic addition and subtraction, and yet most of us have experienced the frustration of an account that won't balance. Why? There are several factors.

Rush, Rush, Rush

Do you ever get in a hurry and forget to record the proper amount? We all have experienced being in this long line of impatient people at the grocery store, and we are scared to death that someone might have to wait thirty seconds longer while I record my check. Then when I get home, I can't remember the right amount. I know; I have done it. Or sometimes we record the checks, but we never bring the balance forward. Maybe we don't want to know how low it is. I have seen people who don't reconcile or balance their checkbooks for six months at a time. We must begin keeping an accurate checkbook.

If you have trouble recording your checks, you can try using duplicate checks. Most banks sell No Carbon Required paper or carbon checks, which automatically record your checks as you write them. You still have to carry your balance forward and reconcile your checkbook to the statement each month, however, but you will know the exact details of each check you write. I use a similar system for my business accounts.

Don't Do This

I know a financial counselor who was trying to help a client with a history of bouncing checks get his checkbook back in balance. As the counselor went through the checkbook, he found neat and precise recording with balances carried forward. He just couldn't find these persistent errors. As he looked he saw $28 for gas, $92 for electricity, $359 for a car payment, $128 for clothes, and $78 for ESP. After reviewing the checkbook carefully, he simply could not find the errors, so he called the client. The counselor said, "My only question is what is ESP?" To which the client replied, "Error Some Place." This is not the way you balance a checkbook. The ESP method does not work.

Budget Busters

You must beware of automatic teller machine cards. These cards are a wonderful convenience, and we use ours for emergency cash withdrawals, but as a cash management tool they are a recordkeeping nightmare and are primarily used for impulse purchases. Even people who do a good job recording their checks forget to post the automatic teller withdrawals. Haven't you seen all the little computer receipts left at the machine? That tells you most people don't record those transactions. It is best to deal in cash. Some simple cash handling techniques explained in upcoming sections will protect you from "budget busters" or impulse decisions at the automatic teller machine. *Never* put a credit card into an ATM machine! Research in *USA Today* stated that the average ATM withdrawal is $53, but when a credit card is used the average rises to $123.[1]

STEP B:
Write Out the Details

In the appendix you will find simple forms that will help you to lay out an accurate monthly cash flow plan. If you will take the time to fill out the forms, you will be well on your way to getting control.

Some categories on the forms require a little explanation, for example, the "Blow" category. You need to plan to blow, waste, or not account for some portion of your money. If you do not plan this, you will do it anyway. The problem isn't that we do not have this category now; the problem is that most people's blow category is their entire plan. A regimented plan that is too tight is not realistic. If you do not allow some cushion in your plan you will fail. Then you will say that plans do not work for you. That's wrong.

A good plan lives and moves—is dynamic—and changes as your life changes. You will need to do a review every month to make adjustments before the month begins. You may have budgeted too little for some areas and be strained, so you will need to adjust. Some areas you will have budgeted too much, and have a surplus; you need to adjust there as well. If you have lived on an ill-prepared budget or no budget at all, it will take you a few minor adjustments to get the plan to a realistic level. The plan is not to complicate your life; on the contrary, when you begin to know where your cash is flowing it will make life easier. You cannot possibly realize you are spending too much on a category if you don't track your spending.

Important, Important

If you do nothing else I have suggested, this little section will change your finances dramatically. Numerous clients have testified of the power of this simple control mechanism. Many writers have recommended the use of this technique, and through practical experience I have found it to be overwhelmingly powerful in the average consumer household. It is the time-honored "envelope system" of cash management, a budgeting system recommended by most good financial counselors.

Items you use a credit card or check for, out of supposed convenience, will likely become budget busters if you continue. For example, suppose you budget $600 per month for groceries, eating out, and prescription drugs. Most people write a check at the grocery store, use a credit card at the restaurant, then another check at the grocery store, and at the end of the month they look back and realize it all adds up to $700. They went over their budget by $100. Unless you keep very careful and cumbersome records throughout the month (and most of you won't) you will usually bust your budget.

Simple as Pie

Implementing the envelope system is simple. If you get paid twice a month, you write a check for $300 to yourself for food on each payday. Then you cash the check and put the $300 cash in an envelope, which you mark "food." As you need to buy food, you take the money from that envelope and from nowhere else.

This does several things for you. It provides you with instantaneous cash management in that you will almost never spend more than allotted. The only way to spend more is to get the money from somewhere else. If you are thinking it has been a hard week and you "deserve" to go out to eat on Friday night, you simply pull out the "food" envelope. You look into the envelope to see if you can afford to do what you need to do. You don't need a complicated bookkeeping system to track your budget. You just look in the envelope.

Emotion Is a Great Manager

Do you remember the power of cash as an emotional negotiating tool? Now you will see the power of that emotion work on you to help you lessen your spending. It is much easier to sign a check or a credit card receipt than it is to lay down cold hard cash to pay for something. When you spend cash it hurts a little bit, so you will end up spending less.

When we started using the envelope system for food, our expenditures on food dropped by over $100 per month. We had been going out more than we needed. Now we do not punish ourselves; we simply manage ourselves. I still enjoy taking my wife out on a date to a nice restaurant, but we just do it by plan now. If we want a romantic dinner on impulse we just check to see if we get cheap romantic or expensive romantic. Romance is more romantic with financial freedom.

You can also use the envelope system for other areas as well. I use it for gasoline and other categories shown on the form system. The categories for which I suggest the envelope system are indicated by a star. I have also suggested the envelope system to use in reverse on small savings items. If you set aside $200 per month for car repairs, maintenance, and tires, you can either deposit that into a savings account or keep the money in an envelope. Then as you need to do repairs, the money is right there, and you can manage the repairs. If you are afraid to have too much cash around the house, I suggest using a categorized savings program, which we will discuss in the forms section.

Estate Planning Is a Must

The last area to address in laying out the details is the paperwork of estate planning. Estate planning from a tax perspective or legal perspective can be very complicated, and you should seek competent legal counsel. I will not address details here. What we do need to talk about is the common sense side of it, though. If you do not have a current will, you should get one now. It is a biological, statistical, and spiritual fact you are going to die. Most of us have avoided completing this little task of writing a will because we think it is morbid or we are superstitious enough to believe that preparing a will hastens our death. That's silly. If you want to control your estate and be responsible to your family, you need to have a current will.

Once you have a will, you should address the major areas of insurance, which are life, health, disability, auto, and homeowner. You should carefully review your coverages and fill in any gaps you identify. Updating your entire insurance program should be done periodically.

Next, you will want to designate a specific place where all the details of your estate are kept. I use a certain drawer in my desk that has a file on each area. My wife knows that if something happens to me, everything she needs to know about our affairs is in that drawer. In addition to that, you should write out detailed instructions to your spouse regarding each area. The last thing a spouse needs to think about in the middle of a crisis is where all the insurance policies are, where the account numbers on savings programs are, and/or where the will is. If you do some simple organization and preparation as a practical estate planning tool, you can prevent confusion or costly mistakes later.

STEP C:
Commit to Your Plan for Ninety Days

You have tried living your life the other way all this time. Why not give these suggestions a real opportunity to take hold? A one-week trial run and the "I-can't-do-it" is not a fair or proper analysis. I am asking you to commit to trying a written plan for ninety days—and I mean *commit*. You commit not to let anything pull you away. If you do not set out with a firm commitment, you will probably give up within the first three weeks. If you will stay with the ninety days, however, I promise that you will work the kinks out and your financial life will never be the same. You will have formed a positive new habit. Successful people know the value of discipline in their lives. I believe committing to your plan for ninety days will change your life. Ninety days would be less than 1 percent of your life, and if you have read this far, you have what it takes to do it.

Just Do It

This chapter has focused on something that few American households have done, namely, developed an accurate, dynamic, written cash management plan. I cannot stress the importance of this enough as a method for getting control of your finances. A written budget does not have to become a huge monster in your mind; it does not have to be overwhelming. I have counseled so many hurting consumers and businesspeople on the brink of bankruptcy, and it makes me ache inside when I know that a simple budget could have saved most of them numerous heartaches. If you will give this a try—commit to this for ninety days—you will be on your way to financial peace.

Thoughts from Sharon . . .

Budgeting, I must admit, is a favorite of mine.

This is how the budget at our home works: Checks are written only to the mortgage company and utilities. All insurance payments are taken from our checking account by preauthorization.

I get paid twice monthly, once on the first and again on the fifteenth. Each time I go to the bank and cash my check, I pick up several money envelopes the bank has provided.

I separate my money into the areas we have budgeted, such as food, clothes, gas, medical, car repairs, and entertainment. I carry only the envelope(s) that I know I will need to spend. Sometimes a certain envelope will run tight. But most of the time I have lots left over.

Dave and I sat down years ago and decided on this budget. The budget is intended to work for our family of five. Changes have to be made since we have a growing family. The food envelope is a good example. As the children grow, we will need to adjust this amount.

Budgeting has brought financial peace to our family. I hope it will do the same for you.

Peace Puppies

1. **Avoid "Stuffitis"—**The Worship of "Stuff"
2. **Plant Seeds—**Give Money Away to Worthy Causes
3. Develop Your Own **"Power over Purchase"**
4. **Find Where You Are Naturally Gifted—**Enjoy Your Work and Work Hard
5. **Live Substantially Below Your Income**
6. **Sacrifice Now** So You Can Have Peace Later
7. **You Can Always Spend More Than You Can Make**
8. **The Borrower Is the Servant to the Lender;** So Beware!
9. **Check Your Credit Report** at Least Once Every Two Years
10. **Handle Credit Report Corrections Yourself**
11. Realize That the Best Way for Delinquent Debt to Be Paid Is for You, Not Collectors, to **Control Your Financial Destiny**
12. **You Must Save Money** (the Power of Compound Interest)
13. Use the **"Keep It Simple, Stupid"** Rule of Investing
14. **Only People Who Like Dog Food Don't Save for Retirement**
15. **Always Save with Pretax Dollars—**It Is the Best Deal the Government Gives You
16. **Learn Basic Negotiating** Skills for Great Buys
17. **Learn Where to Find Great Buys** (the Treasure Hunt)
18. **You Must Have Patience** to Get Great Buys
19. **Singles Get Self-Accountability from the Written Plan**
20. **Singles Should Look for a Money Mentor for Advice and Accountability**
21. **Singles Beware of the Impulse Monster; He Will Eat You Alive**
22. **Men and Women View Money Differently, So Be Sensitive to Differences**
23. **Opposites Attract in Marriage, So Work Together for Maximum Wisdom**

24. **When You Agree on Spending, You Will Experience Fabulous Unity in Your Marriage**
25. **Teach Children to Work, Spend Wisely, Save, and Give**
26. **The Most Powerful Legacy You Can Leave Is Wise, Competent Children**
27. **Giving Loved Ones All the Money They Request May Not Be Best for Them**
28. **Making Decisions Based on Fear of Reprisal Can Be a Sign of Codependence**
29. **Be Strong Enough to Help Others and Strong Enough Not To**
30. **Listen to Your Spouse's Counsel** (Women's Intuition)
31. There Are Few "Old" Fools—**Seek Experienced Counsel**
32. **You Must Keep Your Checkbook on a Timely Basis**
33. Lay Out the Written Details of a **Cash Management Plan**
34. **Commit** to Your Plan for Ninety Days

CHAPTER TWENTY

Do It Daily

You must consciously prioritize your life every day. Most of us need to do this very practical exercise in the morning. Yes, I am saying you should get up thirty minutes earlier. When you get up, you can spend some time in the quiet of the morning assessing where you are and where you want to be. Most of us have grown up in an alarm clock society where we leap out of bed and run through the shower straight to the car, where we drink our first cup of coffee and put on our tie or makeup on the way to work, barely arriving at our place of employment on time. When I sit in traffic, I am always amazed at the number of people who have become fairly good drivers while using their knees to steer so they can eat breakfast and get dressed on the way to work!

Thinking Changes Things

You can not only dramatically affect your financial life by having a quiet time early in the morning, but it will affect your career and your spiritual condition positively as well. In days past America was largely an agricultural society, and we kept different hours. My grandfather will still get up from his chair at 8:30 P.M. and say, "Honey, we are going to have to go to bed so these folks can go home." He was raised in a household where you got up at sunrise, worked hard physically all day, and then went to bed early.

We do what we really want to do. If you truly want to change certain areas of your life to avoid pain and then prosper, you will have to try new ways of doing things. You have probably experienced having planned an exciting Saturday—one for which you had to wake up early—and you wake up thirty minutes before your alarm clock goes off. It is amazing how your mind and body will cooperate for something you really want to do.

Take the Time

If you want to have time to consciously prioritize your life daily, you will make the necessary changes in your lifestyle to accommodate that few minutes of serenity each day. You can spend your quiet time learning from your past by review, as well as thinking where you need to be in five years personally, with your family, and in your career. This time of reflection will cause you to make adjustments in all these areas of your life.

You can also search out your spiritual part, since your makeup is more important than just physical and emotional. I spend my time looking to the Lord Jesus Christ daily, and weekly in church, to strengthen and guide my life. You may ask, "What does this have to do with money?" Everything. We are spiritual beings and when you neglect that aspect of your life, you do not run on full power. All areas of your life will be affected, including money. Yes, Christians have money problems too, but they have an extra ability to survive and prosper in the long run.

As you add quiet time and grow spiritually, the quality of your life will improve, and so will your financial condition. The personal and financial growth that these simple little changes in my daily schedule have brought me is immeasurable. My day starts under control, and so when the torpedoes hit, as they often do, I am ready. I am ready because I am not alone.

Thoughts from Sharon . . .

I know that prioritizing daily activities will show improvements in my life. I must admit, however, that I could improve this area of my life. Don't misunderstand me. I'm organized, but a little more wouldn't hurt. Remember how Dave talks about the Lord giving us spouses that are oppo-

sue? Well, it's true in our household. I'm just an easy-come, easy-go kind of person.

I believe we all need daily devotions with the Lord. This should be reading the Bible and having daily prayer. I enjoy my quiet time in the morning. By doing this early, the rest of the day seems to go smoothly. I have found it a good habit to have.

We all need to think about our lives better organized. We can start with positive thoughts, which will then continue throughout our workday.

Peace Puppies

1. **Avoid "Stuffitis"—**The Worship of "Stuff"
2. **Plant Seeds—**Give Money Away to Worthy Causes
3. Develop Your Own **"Power over Purchase"**
4. **Find Where You Are Naturally Gifted—**Enjoy Your Work and Work Hard
5. **Live Substantially Below Your Income**
6. **Sacrifice Now** So You Can Have Peace Later
7. **You Can Always Spend More Than You Can Make**
8. **The Borrower Is the Servant to the Lender;** So Beware!
9. **Check Your Credit Report** at Least Once Every Two Years
10. **Handle Credit Report Corrections Yourself**
11. Realize That the Best Way for Delinquent Debt to Be Paid Is for You, Not Collectors, to **Control Your Financial Destiny**
12. **You Must Save Money** (the Power of Compound Interest)
13. Use the **"Keep It Simple, Stupid"** Rule of Investing
14. **Only People Who Like Dog Food Don't Save for Retirement**
15. **Always Save with Pretax Dollars—**It Is the Best Deal the Government Gives You
16. **Learn Basic Negotiating** Skills for Great Buys
17. **Learn Where to Find Great Buys** (the Treasure Hunt)
18. **You Must Have Patience** to Get Great Buys
19. **Singles Get Self-Accountability from the Written Plan**
20. **Singles Should Look for a Money Mentor for Advice and Accountability**
21. **Singles Beware of the Impulse Monster; He Will Eat You Alive**
22. **Men and Women View Money Differently, So Be Sensitive to Differences**
23. **Opposites Attract in Marriage, So Work Together for Maximum Wisdom**

24. **When You Agree on Spending, You Will Experience Fabulous Unity in Your Marriage**
25. **Teach Children to Work, Spend Wisely, Save, and Give**
26. **The Most Powerful Legacy You Can Leave Is Wise, Competent Children**
27. **Giving Loved Ones All the Money They Request May Not Be Best for Them**
28. **Making Decisions Based on Fear of Reprisal Can Be a Sign of Codependence**
29. **Be Strong Enough to Help Others and Strong Enough Not To**
30. **Listen to Your Spouse's Counsel** (Women's Intuition)
31. There Are Few "Old" Fools—**Seek Experienced Counsel**
32. **You Must Keep Your Checkbook on a Timely Basis**
33. Lay Out the Written Details of a **Cash Management Plan**
34. **Commit** to Your Plan for Ninety Days
35. **Take Time to Prioritize** Your Life Daily
36. **Keep Your Spiritual Life Healthy**

CHAPTER TWENTY-ONE

Baby Steps

THE END OF OUR large day-long seminars leaves people feeling like this book, a bit overwhelmed. They come up to me and say things like, "Great information, but where in the world do I begin?" The movie *What About Bob?*, starring Bill Murray as the crazy patient of the eminent psychiatrist (played by Richard Dreyfuss), gives the formula for beginning. In this film the Doc has written a book called *Baby Steps* outlining his theory to overcome fears, one step at a time. So Bob (Bill Murray) is "baby stepping" onto elevators and past all manner of phobias, just as we need to do to work into our financial plan one step at a time.

Sticks and Steps

Criswell Freeman in his book, *When Life Throws You a Curveball, Hit It*, retells a story from the Tennessee backwoods that gives us the same answer. There once was a strapping young man with muscles that rippled over his whole body who was known as the strongest man in the county. Once he was challenged at the county fair to a test of strength by a skinny old man. The old man bet that he could break a bundle of hickory sticks in two (every good Tennessean knows the strength of hickory) and that the young strong man couldn't. The rash youngster accepted the bet. So a choice number of hickory sticks were tightly bundled and the contest began. The old man sat down to watch the youngster go first and fail. The poor young man was sweating, bruising his knee, and making himself miserable, but alas he was unable to break the sticks. The old man stood slowly, stretched himself, walked over to the bundle, untied it, and broke the sticks one at a time with ease. The old man and his wisdom were the talk of the county fair. That is how you have a great financial situation, one stick (or step) at a time.

The Process of Baby Steps

The order of implementation is what you are after—how to prioritize the process. Here is the process to work through with bonus money, money from the sale of unwanted items, gifts, or even cash available monthly to attack the plan. *Do not* cash in retirement pretax savings early to get out of debt or use in this process; the penalties and taxes are horrible. However, you should temporarily stop adding to retirement plans or investments until you reach the correct Baby Step.

Another question we are frequently asked is this: "What about giving or tithing? Where does that fit in priority?" You will have to decide that for yourself. My personal decision was to tithe first, since first fruits are mentioned over twenty times in Scripture. I have met with many couples who had to choose between giving and necessities. I refuse to put a guilt trip on you; I want you to decide.

Baby Step One

The first step is pay minimum on everything until you get $1,000 in savings. Go crazy and get this money in the first month of your plan. This savings is the first level of the emergency fund to protect you from little emergencies. If your income is very low you may settle for $500 or if your income is over $70,000 you might use $2,000. Remember, this first level fund is *only* for emergencies.

Baby Step Two

Now is the time for killing all debt. Implement the debt snowball, and pay off all personal debt except your home. (See forms section.) Get mad and stay mad until you get out. Remember, there is no energy in logic, only in emotion.

Baby Step Three

At this point, the only debt you have is your home. So now it should be easy to save the rest of your emergency fund. The correct amount is three to six months of your expenses. Keep this money in a simple money market or bank account, but do no investing with this money. It is only to protect.

Baby Step Four

Save 15 percent of your gross household income in retirement plans. You should begin with 401(k)s or 403(b)s up through the match, then fully fund Roth IRAs. If your 401(k) or 403(b) doesn't match then begin with Roth IRAs. These should all be invested in good growth stock mutual funds (see mutual fund chapter). The total saved in all plans should not be more than 15 percent of income at this Baby Step. At this Baby Step you should also review all your insurance to make sure you have enough coverage of all types. Also, with that emergency fund in place, it is easy to have $500 or $1,000 deductibles, which will drastically lower your premiums.

Baby Step Five

Now and only now is it time to start college funds. You feel guilty—I know—but don't you dare do college funding until you get the first four steps completed. I know those little brown eyes make your blood run cold when you know that the college fund isn't there, but the only way to build a strong house is to lay the proper foundation first, and guilt is not a building block. Just let those little brown eyes be a motivator to run—I mean, sprint—to this step.

Baby Step Six

I love this one. It is now time to pay all the extra you can scrape together to pay your house off early. It may be two, three, even four years to get to this step, but when you do you will be able to knock that house debt off very quickly.

Baby Step Seven

Let's get rich, so rich that we spend our time trying to give it all away. With no payments and great basic savings plans in place, there is nothing left to do but build wealth and give it away. Using real estate, more mutual funds, variable annuities (for the tax deferral), and opportunity money, you can now be the rich getting richer. When that $100,000 deal can be bought for $50,000, you will be there with the cash. Welcome aboard.

A Bundle Broken

The formula for success used by thousands of our clients, radio listeners, and seminar participants was just laid out for you. Now what will you do? Will you try to cheat and sidestep a step? I hope not because the penalty in this game for cheating is going back two steps for every step sidestepped. All broke people think there is a short cut, and the rich, who remain rich, know differently. A word picture from Gary Smalley applies here. Personal finance is not a microwave; it is a crock pot. Pretend that your climb to financial security is like that waterfall my wife and I climbed in Hawaii one year. We got to the top over those very slippery rocks, but we did it by taking one careful, slow step at a time. If you try running up that path, you will find yourself at the bottom with broken bones and bruised egos.

What will it be like to have $10,000 just for emergencies? What will it be like to have no debt? What will it be like to have your retirement adequately funded monthly? What will it be like to have your kids' college being funded monthly? What will it be like having all your insurance in place, knowing your family is protected from financial disaster? What will it be like to give money like crazy to your church and other worthy causes?

What will it be like? Financial Peace.

Thoughts from Sharon . . .

Learning to walk. What an adventurous time it is as we watch small babies take one step at a time. As these babies step forward, will they fall? Yes, of course. They will often have scratched knees and bruised arms.

Some will cry; some will laugh. Some will sit. Some will start again only after their confidence is built up again. As we encourage them, they will jump up and continue walking . . . one step at a time.

Dave's Seven Baby Steps program can help you achieve financial peace. Just as a child does, you will eventually walk.

Peace Puppies

1. **Avoid "Stuffitis"—**The Worship of "Stuff"
2. **Plant Seeds—**Give Money Away to Worthy Causes
3. Develop Your Own **"Power over Purchase"**
4. **Find Where You Are Naturally Gifted—**Enjoy Your Work and Work Hard
5. **Live Substantially Below Your Income**
6. **Sacrifice Now** So You Can Have Peace Later
7. **You Can Always Spend More Than You Can Make**
8. **The Borrower Is the Servant to the Lender;** So Beware!
9. **Check Your Credit Report** at Least Once Every Two Years
10. **Handle Credit Report Corrections Yourself**
11. Realize That the Best Way for Delinquent Debt to Be Paid Is for You, Not Collectors, to **Control Your Financial Destiny**
12. **You Must Save Money** (the Power of Compound Interest)
13. Use the **"Keep It Simple, Stupid"** Rule of Investing
14. **Only People Who Like Dog Food Don't Save for Retirement**
15. **Always Save with Pretax Dollars—**It Is the Best Deal the Government Gives You
16. **Learn Basic Negotiating** Skills for Great Buys
17. **Learn Where to Find Great Buys** (the Treasure Hunt)
18. **You Must Have Patience** to Get Great Buys
19. **Singles Get Self-Accountability from the Written Plan**
20. **Singles Should Look for a Money Mentor for Advice and Accountability**
21. **Singles Beware of the Impulse Monster; He Will Eat You Alive**
22. **Men and Women View Money Differently, So Be Sensitive to Differences**
23. **Opposites Attract in Marriage, So Work Together for Maximum Wisdom**

24. **When You Agree on Spending, You Will Experience Fabulous Unity in Your Marriage**
25. **Teach Children to Work, Spend Wisely, Save, and Give**
26. **The Most Powerful Legacy You Can Leave Is Wise, Competent Children**
27. **Giving Loved Ones All the Money They Request May Not Be Best for Them**
28. **Making Decisions Based on Fear of Reprisal Can Be a Sign of Codependence**
29. **Be Strong Enough to Help Others and Strong Enough Not To**
30. **Listen to Your Spouse's Counsel** (Women's Intuition)
31. There Are Few "Old" Fools—**Seek Experienced Counsel**
32. **You Must Keep Your Checkbook on a Timely Basis**
33. Lay Out the Written Details of a **Cash Management Plan**
34. **Commit** to Your Plan for Ninety Days
35. **Take Time to Prioritize** Your Life Daily
36. **Keep Your Spiritual Life Healthy**
37. **Take Baby Steps—**Prioritize Your Plan and Move Slowly

CHAPTER TWENTY-TWO

The End . . . or Just the Beginning?

WELL, NOW IT IS TIME. It is time for you to decide. Are you a man or a mouse? Are you a woman or a wimp? Are you going to change the way you do things, or are you going to put this book on the shelf to collect dust with all the other self-help books? We human beings resist change, and it takes a conscious and determined effort to make even the slightest changes in our lives.

Nobody Is Perfect

I do not do all the things suggested in the previous pages perfectly. But I do continually make myself aware of what needs to be done and do the best I can at each area. Believe me, a 25 percent improvement in each area will change your life dramatically. It takes time to implement changes in all these areas. It took me some time, but with each change it gets easier. One day you will suddenly realize that you are getting under control! That is the way you eat a whole elephant, one bite at a time. Over time and with conscious effort, I have implemented these principles in my life to about the 90 percent implementation level. Things are really starting to get *fun*.

You really do not have a choice; either you will start controlling your money, or it will forever control you. You can do it! You need to get a tight grip and hold on because you are in for a thrilling ride.

People consider me a strong person with strong opinions, but even I had a hard time getting started and staying on track with making these life-changing decisions. These decisions call for sacrifice, discipline, and patience—three tough words.

Lessons Learned

I have been to the top and then the bottom and back again financially, and I know whatever you are facing you can survive. No matter what you gain or lose in material goods, you can never have talent and hope taken from you, unless you surrender it. I must tell you as we close that there is no way within my own strength that I could have survived learning these lessons the hard way. Only through the power of Christ who strengthens me was this possible.

We have been discussing "peace" and how to attain financial "peace" at length. In our context, this "peace" comes from better manipulation of variables outside ourselves. Using the peace puppies, you can achieve that type of "peace," but you will never find real "peace" from any amount of manipulation of earthly "stuff." The only real "peace" is the "peace that passes all understanding" through Christ. I never found true contentment, true "peace," through any method or formula—until I found Him.

You can learn from the pain and experience of one who has been there and one who has witnessed too many others in their own predicament. You do not have to learn the hard way. If you review these principles as an ongoing guide, you can use them to change your life!

Thoughts from Sharon . . .

I hope as you have read this book that you are or will be well on the road to finding financial peace.

The security and joy of knowing that one day we can all accomplish this goal is overwhelming. As you work toward accomplishing this goal, I pray that the joy of the Lord will fill your hearts. With the Lord's help all things can and will be accomplished. When we need strength, He will be the one to lift us up in that time of need. We must look to Him for answers.

Dave and I have not yet accomplished everything we want. We sometimes feel we have a long road ahead. We know that road ahead will occasionally be rough and bumpy, but we must keep focused. By doing so, we hope to find more love, joy, and peace. I hope you can do the same.

Peace Puppies

1. **Avoid "Stuffitis"—**The Worship of "Stuff"
2. **Plant Seeds—**Give Money Away to Worthy Causes
3. Develop Your Own **"Power over Purchase"**
4. **Find Where You Are Naturally Gifted—**Enjoy Your Work and Work Hard
5. **Live Substantially Below Your Income**
6. **Sacrifice Now** So You Can Have Peace Later
7. **You Can Always Spend More Than You Can Make**
8. **The Borrower Is the Servant to the Lender;** So Beware!
9. **Check Your Credit Report** at Least Once Every Two Years
10. **Handle Credit Report Corrections Yourself**
11. Realize That the Best Way for Delinquent Debt to Be Paid Is for You, Not Collectors, to **Control Your Financial Destiny**
12. **You Must Save Money** (the Power of Compound Interest)
13. Use the **"Keep It Simple, Stupid"** Rule of Investing
14. **Only People Who Like Dog Food Don't Save for Retirement**
15. **Always Save with Pretax Dollars—**It Is the Best Deal the Government Gives You
16. **Learn Basic Negotiating** Skills for Great Buys
17. **Learn Where to Find Great Buys** (the Treasure Hunt)
18. **You Must Have Patience** to Get Great Buys
19. **Singles Get Self-Accountability from the Written Plan**
20. **Singles Should Look for a Money Mentor for Advice and Accountability**
21. **Singles Beware of the Impulse Monster; He Will Eat You Alive**
22. **Men and Women View Money Differently, So Be Sensitive to Differences**
23. **Opposites Attract in Marriage, So Work Together for Maximum Wisdom**

24. **When You Agree on Spending, You Will Experience Fabulous Unity in Your Marriage**
25. **Teach Children to Work, Spend Wisely, Save, and Give**
26. **The Most Powerful Legacy You Can Leave Is Wise, Competent Children**
27. **Giving Loved Ones All the Money They Request May Not Be Best for Them**
28. **Making Decisions Based on Fear of Reprisal Can Be a Sign of Codependence**
29. **Be Strong Enough to Help Others and Strong Enough Not To**
30. **Listen to Your Spouse's Counsel** (Women's Intuition)
31. There Are Few "Old" Fools—**Seek Experienced Counsel**
32. **You Must Keep Your Checkbook on a Timely Basis**
33. Lay Out the Written Details of a **Cash Management Plan**
34. **Commit** to Your Plan for Ninety Days
35. **Take Time to Prioritize** Your Life Daily
36. **Keep Your Spiritual Life Healthy**
37. **Take Baby Steps—**Prioritize Your Plan and Move Slowly

APPENDICES

Financial Management Forms

WELCOME TO THE WONDERFUL WORLD of "cash flow management." Filling out these few forms and following your new plan will change your financial future. The first time you fill out the forms will be tough and take time. But when you come back for another look, you will get faster and the forms will be easier—so you should not let this discourage you.

The length and the amount of detail may seem overwhelming. However, I have found that if you don't have the detail as a track to run on, you will always leave something out. Can you guess what happens then? If you leave out items that you are really spending, you will crash your plan and have an excuse to quit. So you need to concentrate and complete all the forms this one time.

After you have filled out the whole set once, you only need to do Work Sheet 7 or Work Sheet 8 (whichever is applicable) once per month, which should take about thirty minutes. Work Sheet 5 can be done once per quarter, and since you will see only minor changes from one quarter to the next, you can estimate about one hour per quarter to update. The entire pack should be redone once a year or when any large positive or negative financial event occurs (such as Aunt Ethel's leaving you $10,000 in her will).

Once you have made it through this planning process the first time, you should be able to manage your finances in thirty minutes per month—plus what it takes to write checks and balance your checkbook.

One note: Be sure that you keep your promises on Work Sheet 1 and share them with your spouse, if you are married.

Work Sheet 1

Major Components of a Healthy Financial Plan

	ACTION NEEDED	ACTION DATE
Written Cash Flow Plan	______________	________
Will and/or Estate Plan	______________	________
Debt Reduction Plan	______________	________
Tax Reduction Plan	______________	________
Emergency Funding	______________	________
Retirement Funding	______________	________
College Funding	______________	________
Charitable Giving	______________	________
Teach My Children	______________	________
Life Insurance	______________	________
Health Insurance	______________	________
Disability Insurance	______________	________
Auto Insurance	______________	________
Homeowner's Insurance	______________	________

I, ______________________________, a responsible adult, do hereby swear to take the above stated actions by the above stated dates to financially secure the well-being of my family and myself. (Copy to Spouse)

Signed: ______________________________ Date: ____________

Consumer Equity Work Sheet

ITEM / DESCRIBE	VALUE	– DEBT	= EQUITY
Real Estate ________	________	________	________
Real Estate ________	________	________	________
Car ________	________	________	________
Car ________	________	________	________
Cash On Hand	________	________	________
Checking Account	________	________	________
Checking Account	________	________	________
Savings Account	________	________	________
Savings Account	________	________	________
Money Market Account	________	________	________
Mutual Funds	________	________	________
Retirement Plan	________	________	________
Stocks or Bonds	________	________	________
Cash Value (Insurance)	________	________	________
Household Items	________	________	________
Jewelry	________	________	________
Antiques	________	________	________
Boat	________	________	________
Unsecured Debt (Negative)	________	________	________
Credit Card Debt (Negative)	________	________	________
Other ________	________	________	________
Other ________	________	________	________
Other ________	________	________	________
TOTAL	________	________	________

Work Sheet 3

Income Sources

SOURCE	AMOUNT	PERIOD / DESCRIBE
Salary 1		
Salary 2		
Salary 3		
Bonus		
Self-Employment		
Interest Income		
Dividend Income		
Royalty Income		
Rents		
Notes		
Alimony		
Child Support		
AFDC		
Unemployment		
Social Security		
Pension		
Annuity		
Disability Income		
Cash Gifts		
Trust Fund		
Other ________		
Other ________		
Other ________		
Other ________		
TOTAL		

Lump Sum Payment Planning

Payments you make on a non-monthly basis can be budget busters, if you do not plan for them. Here you will convert these to a monthly basis for use on Work Sheet 5. Then you will set money aside monthly to avoid strain or borrowing when these events occur. If an item here is already paid monthly, enter NA. If you make a payment quarterly, then annualize it for this work sheet.

ITEM NEEDED	ANNUAL AMOUNT		MONTHLY AMOUNT
Real Estate Taxes	________	÷ 12 =	________
Homeowner's Ins.	________	÷ 12 =	________
Home Repairs	________	÷ 12 =	________
Replace Furniture	________	÷ 12 =	________
Medical Bills	________	÷ 12 =	________
Health Insurance	________	÷ 12 =	________
Life Insurance	________	÷ 12 =	________
Disability Insurance	________	÷ 12 =	________
Car Insurance	________	÷ 12 =	________
Car Repair/Tags	________	÷ 12 =	________
Replace Car	________	÷ 12 =	________
Clothing	________	÷ 12 =	________
Tuition	________	÷ 12 =	________
Bank Note	________	÷ 12 =	________
IRS (Self-Employed)	________	÷ 12 =	________
Vacation	________	÷ 12 =	________
Gifts (inc. Christmas)	________	÷ 12 =	________
Other ________	________	÷ 12 =	________
Other ________	________	÷ 12 =	________

Work Sheet 5 Instructions

Every dollar of your income should be allocated to some category on this monthly cash flow plan. Money "left over" should be put back into a category even if you make up a new category. You should make spending decisions ahead of time. Almost every category (except debt) should have some dollar amount in it. For example, if you do not plan to replace the furniture, when you need to do so in the future your finances will be strained and you will need to borrow. Plan for that expense now by saving for it. I have actually had people tell me that they can do without clothing. (Oh, come on!) Be careful too in your zeal to make the numbers work that you don't substitute the urgent for the important.

Fill in the amount for each subcategory under "Subtotal" and then the total for each main category under "Total." As you go through your first month, fill in the "Actually Spent" column with your real expenses or the savings you had for that area. If there is a substantial difference in the plan versus the reality, something has to change. You will either have to adjust the amount allocated to that area up and another down, or you will have to better control your spending in that area.

In the column "% Take-Home Pay," write in the percentage of your total take-home pay that you spent on a particular category, such as "Housing." Then you can compare your percentages with those on Work Sheet 6 to determine if you need to consider adjusting your lifestyle.

An asterisk (*) beside an item means that you should use the "envelope system" (see pages 257–58).

IMPORTANT (1): Emergency Fund should get all the savings until three to six months of expenses have been saved.

NOTE: Savings should be increased as you get closer to being debt free.

HINT: By saving early for Christmas and other gifts, you can get great buys and give better gifts for the same money.

Monthly Cash Flow Plan

	BUDGETED			
ITEM	SUB-TOTAL	TOTAL	ACTUALLY SPENT	% of TAKE-HOME PAY
CHARITABLE GIFTS		______	______	______
SAVING				
Emergency Fund (1)	______		______	
Retirement Fund	______		______	
College Fund	______	______	______	______
HOUSING				
First Mortgage	______		______	
Second Mortgage	______		______	
Real Estate Taxes	______		______	
Homeowner's Ins.	______		______	
Repairs or Mnt. Fee	______		______	
Replace Furniture	______		______	
Other	______	______	______	______
UTILITIES				
Electricity	______		______	
Water	______		______	
Gas	______		______	
Phone	______		______	
Trash	______		______	
Cable	______	______	______	______
*FOOD				
*Grocery	______		______	
*Restaurants	______	______	______	______
PAGE 1 TOTAL		______	______	

Work Sheet 5 continued

ITEM	BUDGETED SUB-TOTAL	BUDGETED TOTAL	ACTUALLY SPENT	% of TAKE-HOME PAY
TRANSPORTATION				
Car Payment	________		________	
Car Payment	________		________	
*Gas and Oil	________		________	
*Repairs and Tires	________		________	
Car Insurance	________		________	
License and Taxes	________		________	
Car Replacement	________	________	________	________
*CLOTHING				
*Children	________		________	
*Adults	________		________	
*Cleaning/Laundry	________	________	________	________
MEDICAL/HEALTH				
Disability Ins.	________		________	
Health Insurance	________		________	
Doctor Bills	________		________	
Dentist	________		________	
Optometrist	________		________	
Drugs	________	________	________	________
PERSONAL				
Life Insurance	________		________	
Child Care	________		________	
PAGE 2 TOTAL		________	________	

ITEM	BUDGETED SUB-TOTAL	BUDGETED TOTAL	ACTUALLY SPENT	% of TAKE-HOME PAY
PERSONAL *(continued)*				
*Baby-Sitter	______		______	
*Toiletries	______		______	
*Cosmetics	______		______	
*Hair Care	______		______	
Education/Adult	______		______	
School Tuition	______		______	
School Supplies	______		______	
Child Support	______		______	
Alimony	______		______	
Subscriptions	______		______	
Organization Dues	______		______	
Gifts (inc. Christmas)	______		______	
Miscellaneous	______		______	
*BLOW $$	______	______	______	______
RECREATION				
*Entertainment	______		______	
Vacation	______	______	______	______
DEBTS (Hopefully $0)				
Visa 1	______		______	
Visa 2	______		______	
MasterCard 1	______		______	
MasterCard 2	______		______	
PAGE 3 TOTAL		______	______	

Work Sheet 5 continued

ITEM	BUDGETED SUB-TOTAL	BUDGETED TOTAL	ACTUALLY SPENT	% of TAKE-HOME PAY
DEBTS (Hopefully $0) *(continued)*				
American Express	______		______	
DiscoverCard	______		______	
Gas Card 1	______		______	
Gas Card 2	______		______	
Dept. Store Card 1	______		______	
Dept. Store Card 2	______		______	
Finance Co. 1	______		______	
Finance Co. 2	______		______	
Credit Line	______		______	
Student Loan 1	______		______	
Student Loan 2	______		______	
Other ____________	______		______	
Other ____________	______		______	
Other ____________	______		______	
Other ____________	______		______	
Other ____________	______	______	______	______
PAGE 4 TOTAL		______	______	
PAGE 3 TOTAL		______	______	
PAGE 2 TOTAL		______	______	
PAGE 1 TOTAL		______	______	
GRAND TOTAL		______	______	
TOTAL INCOME	minus	______	______	
DIFFERENCE		Zero	______	

Recommended Percentages

I have used a compilation of several sources and my own experience to derive the suggested percentage guidelines. However, these are only recommended percentages and will change dramatically if you have a very high or very low income. For instance, if you have a very low income, your necessities percentages will be high. If you have a high income, your necessities will be a lower percentage of income and hopefully savings (not debt) will be higher than recommended.

ITEM	ACTUAL %	RECOMMENDED %
Charitable Gifts	______________	10–15%
Saving	______________	5–10%
Housing	______________	25–35%
Utilities	______________	5–10%
Food	______________	5–15%
Transportation	______________	10–15%
Clothing	______________	2–7%
Medical/Health	______________	5–10%
Personal	______________	5–10%
Recreation	______________	5–10%
Debts	______________	5–10%

Work Sheet 7 Instructions

This work sheet is where all your work thus far starts giving you some peace. You will implement your Work Sheet 5 information into your life, going from theory to reality, by using Work Sheet 7. (Please note: If you have an irregular income, like self-employment or commissions, you should use Work Sheet 8, after reviewing Work Sheet 7.)

There are four columns to distribute as many as four different incomes within one month. Each column is one pay period. If you are a one-income household and you get paid two times per month, then you will use only two columns. If both spouses work and one is paid weekly and the other every two weeks, add the two paychecks together on the weeks you both get a paycheck, and list the one paycheck on the other two. Date the pay period columns and then enter the income for that period. As you allocate your paycheck to an item, put the remaining balance to the right of the slash. Income for period 1 in our example is $1,000 and we are allocating $100 to "Charitable Giving," leaving $900 to the right of the slash in that same column. Some bills will come out of each pay period and some only on selected pay periods. As an example, you may take "Car Gas" out of every paycheck, but you may pay the electric bill from period 2. You already pay some bills or make payments out of designated checks; now you pay all things from designated checks.

The whole point to this work sheet, which is the culmination of all your monthly planning, is to allocate or "spend" your whole paycheck before you get paid. I don't care where you allocate your money, but you must allocate all of it before you get your check. Now all the tense, crisis-like symptoms have been removed because you planned. No more management by crisis or impulse. Those who tend to be impulsive should just allocate more to the "Blow" category. At least you are now doing it on purpose and not by default. The last blank that you make an entry in should have a 0 to the right of the slash, showing you have allocated your whole check.

Work Sheet 7

Sample Allocated Spending Plan

PAY PERIOD:	________	________	________	________
ITEM:				
INCOME	________	________	________	________
CHARITABLE	____/____	____/____	____/____	____/____
SAVING				
Emergency Fund	____/____	____/____	____/____	____/____
Retirement Fund	____/____	____/____	____/____	____/____
College Fund	____/____	____/____	____/____	____/____
HOUSING				
First Mortgage	____/____	____/____	____/____	____/____
Second Mortgage	____/____	____/____	____/____	____/____
Real Estate Taxes	____/____	____/____	____/____	____/____
Homeowner's Ins.	____/____	____/____	____/____	____/____
Repairs/Mnt. Fees	____/____	____/____	____/____	____/____
Replace Furniture	____/____	____/____	____/____	____/____
Other ________	____/____	____/____	____/____	____/____
UTILITIES				
Electricity	____/____	____/____	____/____	____/____
Water	____/____	____/____	____/____	____/____
Gas	____/____	____/____	____/____	____/____
Phone	____/____	____/____	____/____	____/____

UTILITIES *(continued)*				
Trash	___/___	___/___	___/___	___/___
Cable	___/___	___/___	___/___	___/___
*FOOD				
*Grocery	___/___	___/___	___/___	___/___
*Restaurants	___/___	___/___	___/___	___/___
TRANSPORTATION				
Car Payment	___/___	___/___	___/___	___/___
Car Payment	___/___	___/___	___/___	___/___
*Gas & Oil	___/___	___/___	___/___	___/___
*Repairs & Tires	___/___	___/___	___/___	___/___
Car Insurance	___/___	___/___	___/___	___/___
License & Taxes	___/___	___/___	___/___	___/___
Car Replacement	___/___	___/___	___/___	___/___
*CLOTHING				
*Children	___/___	___/___	___/___	___/___
*Adults	___/___	___/___	___/___	___/___
*Cleaning/Lndry.	___/___	___/___	___/___	___/___
MEDICAL/HEALTH				
Disability Ins.	___/___	___/___	___/___	___/___
Health Insurance	___/___	___/___	___/___	___/___
Doctor	___/___	___/___	___/___	___/___
Dentist	___/___	___/___	___/___	___/___
Optometrist	___/___	___/___	___/___	___/___
Drugs	___/___	___/___	___/___	___/___

PERSONAL				
Life Insurance	___/___	___/___	___/___	___/___
Child Care	___/___	___/___	___/___	___/___
*Baby-Sitter	___/___	___/___	___/___	___/___
*Toiletries	___/___	___/___	___/___	___/___
*Cosmetics	___/___	___/___	___/___	___/___
*Hair Care	___/___	___/___	___/___	___/___
Education/Adult	___/___	___/___	___/___	___/___
School Tuition	___/___	___/___	___/___	___/___
School Supplies	___/___	___/___	___/___	___/___
Child Support	___/___	___/___	___/___	___/___
Alimony	___/___	___/___	___/___	___/___
Subscriptions	___/___	___/___	___/___	___/___
Organization Dues	___/___	___/___	___/___	___/___
Gifts (inc. Christmas)	___/___	___/___	___/___	___/___
Miscellaneous	___/___	___/___	___/___	___/___
*BLOW $$	___/___	___/___	___/___	___/___
RECREATION				
*Entertainment	___/___	___/___	___/___	___/___
Vacation	___/___	___/___	___/___	___/___
DEBTS (Hopefully $0)				
Visa 1	___/___	___/___	___/___	___/___
Visa 2	___/___	___/___	___/___	___/___
MasterCard 1	___/___	___/___	___/___	___/___
MasterCard 2	___/___	___/___	___/___	___/___

DEBTS (Hopefully $0)—*continued*

Amer. Express	___/___	___/___	___/___	___/___
DiscoverCard	___/___	___/___	___/___	___/___
Gas Card 1	___/___	___/___	___/___	___/___
Gas Card 2	___/___	___/___	___/___	___/___
Dept. Store Card 1	___/___	___/___	___/___	___/___
Dept. Store Card 2	___/___	___/___	___/___	___/___
Finance Co. 1	___/___	___/___	___/___	___/___
Finance Co. 2	___/___	___/___	___/___	___/___
Credit Line	___/___	___/___	___/___	___/___
Student Loan 1	___/___	___/___	___/___	___/___
Student Loan 2	___/___	___/___	___/___	___/___
Other ________	___/___	___/___	___/___	___/___
Other ________	___/___	___/___	___/___	___/___
Other ________	___/___	___/___	___/___	___/___
Other ________	___/___	___/___	___/___	___/___
Other ________	___/___	___/___	___/___	___/___

Irregular Income Planning

Many of us have irregular incomes. If you are self-employed, as I am, or work on commission or royalties, then planning your expenses is difficult, since you cannot always predict your income. You should, however, still do all the work sheets except Work Sheet 7. Work Sheet 5 will tell you what you have to earn monthly to survive or prosper, and those real numbers are very good for goal setting.

What you must do is to take the items on Work Sheet 5 and prioritize them by importance. Remember, by importance, not urgency. You should ask yourself, "If I have only enough money to pay one thing, what would that be?" Then ask, "If I have only enough money to pay one more thing, what will that be?" And so on down the list. Now, be prepared to stand your ground because things have a way of seeming important when they are not. Saving should be a high priority.

The third column, "Cumulative Amount," is the total of all amounts above that item. So if you get a $2,000 check, you can see how far down your priority list you can go.

ITEM	AMOUNT	CUMULATIVE AMOUNT

Work Sheet 8 continued

ITEM	AMOUNT	CUMULATIVE AMOUNT

Breakdown of Savings

As you save for certain items like furniture, car replacement, home maintenance, or clothes, your savings balance will grow. This sheet is designed to remind you that all of that money is committed to something, not just a Hawaiian vacation on impulse because you are now "rich." Keep up with your breakdown of savings monthly for one quarter at a time.

ITEM	BALANCE BY MONTH:			
Emergency Fund (1)		________	________	________
Retirement Fund		________	________	________
College Fund		________	________	________
Real Estate Taxes		________	________	________
Homeowner's Insurance		________	________	________
Repairs or Mnt. Fee		________	________	________
Replace Furniture		________	________	________
Car Insurance		________	________	________
Car Replacement		________	________	________
Disability Insurance		________	________	________
Health Insurance		________	________	________
Doctor		________	________	________
Dentist		________	________	________
Optometrist		________	________	________
Life Insurance		________	________	________
School Tuition		________	________	________
School Supplies		________	________	________
Gifts (inc. Christmas)		________	________	________
Vacation		________	________	________
Other ____________		________	________	________
Other ____________		________	________	________
Other ____________		________	________	________
	TOTAL	________	________	________

Work Sheet 10

The Debt Snowball

List your debts in descending order with the smallest payoff or balance first. Do not be concerned with interest rates or terms unless two debts have similar payoffs; then list the higher interest rate debt first. Paying the little debts off first shows you quick feedback, and you are more likely to stay with the plan.

Redo this work sheet each time you pay off a debt so you can see how close you are getting to freedom. Keep the old work sheets to wallpaper the bathroom in your new debt-free house. The "New Payment" is found by adding all the payments on the debts listed above that item to the payment you are working on, so you have compounding payments which will get you out of debt very quickly. "Payments Remaining" is the number of payments remaining when you get down the snowball to that item. "Cumulative Payments" is the total payments needed, including the snowball, to pay off that item. In other words, this is your running total for "Payments Remaining."

Date: ______________________ Countdown to freedom

Item	Total Payoff	Minimum Pymt.	New Pymt.	Pymts. Remaining	Cumulative Pymts.

Item	Total Payoff	Minimum Pymt.	New Pymt.	Pymts. Remaining	Cumulative Pymts.

Work Sheet 11

Retirement Monthly Planning

In order to retire with some security, you must aim at something. Too many people use the *ready, fire, aim* approach to retirement planning. Your assignment is to determine how much per month you should be saving at 12 percent interest in order to retire at 65 years old with what you need.

If you are saving at 12 percent and inflation is at 4 percent then you are moving ahead of inflation at a net of 8 percent per year. If you invest your nest egg at retirement at 12 percent and want to break even with 4 percent inflation, you will be living on 8 percent income.

STEP ONE:

Annual income (today) you wish to retire on $ ____________

divided by ____.08____

(nest egg needed) equals $ ____________

STEP TWO:

To achieve that nest egg, you will save at 12 percent, netting 8 percent after inflation, so we will target that nest egg using 8 percent.

____________ × ____________ = ____________

Nest Egg Needed   Factor Monthly   Savings Needed

8% factors (select the one that matches your age)

Age	Years to Save	Factor
25	40	.000286
30	35	.000436
35	30	.000671
40	25	.001051
45	20	.001698
50	15	.002890
55	10	.005466
60	5	.013610

NOTE: If you have any doubts about saving now, take a look at what happens if you delay saving for five or ten years.

Pro Rata Plan

If you cannot pay your creditors what they request, you should treat them all fairly and the same. You should pay even the ones who are jerks, and pay everyone as much as you can. Many creditors will accept a written plan and cut special deals with you as long as you are communicating, maybe even overcommunicating, and sending them something. We have had clients using this plan who have sent only $2 and have survived literally for years.

Pro rata means their share—the percentage of your total debt they are owed determines how much you send them. You send the check with a budget and this work sheet attached each month even if the creditor says they will not accept it.

Item	Total Payoff	÷ Total Debt	= Percent	× Disposable Income	= New Payments
		÷	=.	×	=
		÷	=.	×	=
		÷	=.	×	=
		÷	=.	×	=
		÷	=.	×	=
		÷	=.	×	=
		÷	=.	×	=
		÷	=.	×	=
		÷	=.	×	=
		÷	=.	×	=
		÷	=.	×	=
		÷	=.	×	=
		÷	=.	×	=
		÷	=.	×	=
		÷	=.	×	=
		÷	=.	×	=

Work Sheet 12 continued

Item	Total Payoff	÷ Total Debt	= Percent	× Disposable Income	= New Payments
		÷	=.	×	=
		÷	=.	×	=
		÷	=.	×	=
		÷	=.	×	=
		÷	=.	×	=
		÷	=.	×	=
		÷	=.	×	=
		÷	=.	×	=
		÷	=.	×	=
		÷	=.	×	=
		÷	=.	×	=
		÷	=.	×	=
		÷	=.	×	=
		÷	=.	×	=
		÷	=.	×	=
		÷	=.	×	=
		÷	=.	×	=
		÷	=.	×	=
		÷	=.	×	=
		÷	=.	×	=
		÷	=.	×	=
		÷	=.	×	=
		÷	=.	×	=
		÷	=.	×	=
		÷	=.	×	=
		÷	=.	×	=
		÷	=.	×	=

National Credit Bureaus

TRW CREDIT BUREAU (800) 392-1122
Copies are $7 each. Free copies are available if you have been denied credit in the past 60 days and the creditor used TRW's services.

EQUIFAX CREDIT BUREAU (800) 685-1111
Copies of your personal credit file are available for a small fee (up to $8) depending on your state of residence. Free copies are available if you have been denied credit in the past 60 days and the creditor used Equifax's services.

TRANSUNION CREDIT BUREAU (800) 916-8800
Copies of your personal credit file are available for $15 each depending on your state of residence. Free copies are available if you have been denied credit in the past 60 days and the creditor used TransUnion's services.

TO COMPLAIN:
Federal Trade Commission Headquarters (202) 326-2222
6th and Pennsylvania Avenue, N.W.
Washington, D.C. 20580

TO STOP OR DISCOURAGE PRE-APPROVED CREDIT CARD OFFERS:
Many companies market consumer products and services by mail. Millions of people take advantage of these direct marketing opportunities because it is a convenient way to shop. If you prefer not to receive direct marketing mailings, you can write to: Direct Marketing Association, Mail Preference Service, P.O. Box 9008, Farmingdale, New York 11735-9008. Include your complete name, full address, Social Security number, and signature. The Direct Marketing Association will have your name removed from these lists.

Many credit card companies and lenders utilize Equifax's database to offer pre-approved credit. If you prefer not to receive pre-approved offers, please notify: Equifax Options, P.O. Box 740123, Atlanta, GA 30374-0123. Include your complete name, full address, Social Security number, and signature. Equifax will remove your name from the lists it provides and share your request with the other two major credit-reporting agencies.

Sample Letter #1
Credit Bureau Cleanup

[Date] ________________

[From]

____

____

____

[To]

________________________________ ***Credit Bureau***

____

____

RE: ___________________________________

Dear ___________________________ :

In reviewing the attached credit bureau report issued by your agency, I have detected an error regarding the following account(s) in that it is reported inaccurately.

Company Name: _____________________________

Account Number: ____________________________

Under the provision set forth in the 1977 Federal Fair Credit Reporting Act, I hereby request that your agency prove to me in writing the accuracy of the reporting of this account. Under the terms of the Act and succeeding court cases, you have 30 days to prove such accuracy or remove the account entirely from my report and I ask that you do so.

You will note that this letter was sent by certified mail and that I expect a response within the said 30-day period. Should I not hear promptly from you I *will* follow up with whatever action is necessary to cause my report to be corrected.

Please feel free to call me if you have any questions. My home phone number is _____________ and my office number is ______________ .

Sincerely,

____

Sample Letter #2
Creditor Calls at Work

[Date] ________________

[From]

____

____

____

[To]

____

____

____

RE: ___________________________________

Dear ___________________________ :

I am writing to formally request that your firm (or any agency hired by your firm) no longer contact me at my place of employment:

____ .

My employer requests that calls such as yours must cease. Under the terms of the 1977 Federal Fair Debt Collection Practices Act, I formally demand that all such calls to my place of employment cease. You will please take note that this letter was sent by certified mail so I have proof that you are in receipt of this letter should legal action against you become necessary on this matter.

I am willing to pay the debt I owe you and I will be in touch soon to work out arrangements.

Feel free to contact me at my home between ___________ A.M. and ___________ P.M. at the following number ___________________ or by mail at my home address:

____

____

____

Please give this matter the attention it deserves.

Sincerely,

____

Sample Letter #3
Cease and Desist

[Date] ________________

[From]

____

____

____

VIA: Certified Mail, Return Receipt Requested

[To]

____

____

____

RE: ___________________________________

Dear ___________________________ :

This letter will serve as your legal notice under federal law that regulates the activities of collection agencies and their legal representatives.

You are hereby notified under provisions of Public Law 95-109, Section 805-C, THE FAIR DEBT COLLECTION PRACTICES ACT, to CEASE AND DESIST in any and all attempts to collect the above debt.

Your failure to do so WILL result in charges being filed against you with the state and federal regulatory agencies empowered with enforcement.

Please be further warned that if ANY derogatory information is placed on any credit reports after receipt of this notice, it too will result in action being taken against you.

PLEASE GIVE THIS MATTER THE ATTENTION IT DESERVES.

Yours truly,

____

Notes

Every effort has been made to give complete bibliographic information for all references. If the reader desires more specific information regarding any source, he or she should contact the author.

Chapter 2: Enough of Anything Is Too Much

1. "How to Manage Your Money," The Christian Financial Concepts Series (Chicago: Moody Press, 1975).
2. Jeff Blyskal, "Loans," *The Consumer Reports Money Book* (New York: Consumers Union of United States, Inc., 1995), chapter 3.
3. "Debt's Making Unhappy Homes," *Cardflash,* status report cited by Florida-based Consolidated Credit Counseling Services.
4. Dearborn Trade, *Fast Facts on Consumer Credit Problems and Bankruptcy*.
5. Anne R. Carey and Bob Laird, "Worried About Getting By," Marist Institute for Public Opinion in *USA Today* (n.d.).
6. "U.S. Mortgage Debt in Billions," status report of Board of Governors of the Federal Reserve System, www.federalreserve.gov.
7. "Foreclosure," *Bank Rate Monitor* status report.
8. American Bankruptcy Institute, 44 Canal Center Plaza, Suite 404, Alexandria, VA.
9. Ibid.
10. Wade Lambert, "The New Faces of Personal Bankruptcy: Baby Boomers," *Wall Street Journal* (n.d.), B–1.

11. "Consumer Credit Advertising," Jupiter Media Metrix's Adrelevance Service, status report.

Chapter 6: Career Choice

1. Robin Fulton Manly, "Monday mornings bring on heart attacks," *Los Angeles Times Syndicate* (n.d.).

Chapter 8: Dumping Debt

1. Bobby Eklund and Terry Austin, *"Partners with God! Bible Truths About Giving"* (Nashville, TN: Convention Press, 1994).
2. Gary Levin, "Aggressive credit cards to go on ad spending spree," *Advertising Age,* vol. 65 (Sept. 28, 1994), 40.
3. "Credit Card Mail Solicitations," BAIGlobal, status report.
4. Melanie Wells, "Kirshenbaum warms up to direct," *Advertising Age,* vol. 65 (Aug. 15, 1994), 25.
5. "Teach your kid the facts of credit," *Medical Economics,* vol. 71 (Nov. 7, 1994), 85–86.
6. Kerry Dolan, "Gettin a charge out of rock 'n' roll," *Forbes,* vol. 154 (Dec. 19, 1994), 302.
7. Lisa Renee Brown, "Country on Credit," *Nashville Banner* (July 6, 1995), A–2.
8. Jeff Blyskal, "Loans," *The Consumer Reports Money Book* (New York: Consumers Union of United States, Inc., 1995), 32.
9. Jeff Blyskal, "Charge Cards," *The Consumer Reports Money Book, 1995,* 50.
10. Kevin T. Higgins, "Bottom fishing," *Credit Card Management,* vol. 6 (Jan. 1994), 62–71.
11. Status Report, "Credit Daze," *Smart Money* (March 1995), cited by Ram Research Corp.
12. "Average Cardholder Balance," CardTrack, status report cited by RAM Research Corp.
13. "Consumer Credit Card Limit," CardWeb, status report cited by CCCS Online Survey.
14. "Number of Consumers with Credit Cards," CardTrack, status report cited by RAM Research Corp.
15. "Sears Credit Cards," CardTrack, status report cited by *The Pittsburgh Post-Gazette,* www.post-gazette.com, *The Wall Street Journal* (n.d.).
16. "American Express Cardholders," Reuters, status report.

17. "Cardholder Average Interest Rate," RAM Research Corp., status report.
18. Robert J. Klein, "When to borrow, when to pay cash," *D & B Reports* (March/April 1993), 63.
19. Anne Willette, "GM Card ringing up food rebates," *USA Today* (n.d.).
20. Status Report, "Credit Daze," *Smart Money* (March 1995), cited by Ram Research Corp.
21. "A reason to scissor some credit cards," *Kiplinger's Personal Financial Magazine* (n.d.).
22. "Buyers: The price is right on used cars," *USA Today* (Jan. 18, 1995), B–1.
23. "Or should you lease instead?" *Consumer Reports* (April 1994), 259.
24. *Smart Money* (October 1994), 106.
25. Vanessa O'Connell, "Am Ex's True Grace Card is a mixed blessing," *Money*, vol. 23 (Nov. 1994), 42.

Chapter 9: Cucumbers, Collectors, and Credit Reports

1. "Credit Report Errors," U.S. Public Interest Research Group, status report.

Chapter 10: Pile Up Plunder

1. "American Savings Rate," NLI Research Institute, status report cited by U.S. Department of Commerce.
2. Robert Sullivan, "An Intimate Portrait: Americans and Their Money," chart, "The Meaning of Money," by Jared Schneidman, *Worth* (June 1994), 61.
3. John Riley and Bob Lair, "Faith in Social Security Falls," citing the Wirthlin Group Poll, *USA Today* (n.d.).
4. "Wealth Creation in America," The Bull & Bear Financial Report, status report.
5. "Financial Planning 101," *Money* (March 1989), 78.

Chapter 11: "KISS" Your Money

1. John R. Dofman, "Toss of the Darts Bests Pros in Stock-Picking Contest," *Wall Street Journal* (n.d.), C–1.
2. Denise Gray, "Credit Life Comes Alive," *Credit Card Management*, 59.
3. Ibid.
4. "Millions Threatened by Financial Ignorance," *Special Report: Personal Economic Summit '93* (Sept. 30–Oct. 2, 1993), 2.

Chapter 12: Of Mice and Mutual Funds

1. "Largest mutual funds," Lipper Analytical Service. As printed in *USA Today* (1995).
2. Consumer Price Index, U.S. Bureau of Labor Statistics.
3. U.S. League of Savings Institutions, The Federal Reserve Board, U.S. Department of Labor Statistics.
4. Lipper Analytical Services, Inc.
5. "The Long Run Perspective," *Stocks, Bonds, Bills, and Inflation, 1994 Yearbook* (Chicago: Ibbotson Assoc., 1994), 41.
6. Anne Willette, "Poll: Only 44% are preparing for retirement," *USA Today* (May 8–11, 1995), 1.
7. "Consumer Savings," CardWeb, status report cited by CCCS Online Survey.
8. "Traditional Pension Plans," *Fortune 100,* status report cited by Watson Wyatt Benefits Consulting Firm.
9. James Alvey, "Skimpy Savings," *Fortune* (Feb. 20, 1995).
10. "The Smart 401K," *Business Week* (July 3, 1995).

Chapter 13: Buy Only Big, Big Bargains

1. Roger Fisher and William Ury, *Getting to Yes: How to Negotiate Agreement Without Giving In* (Chicago: Nightingale Conant).
2. Ibid.
3. "The Best of the Almost-New Cars," *Kiplinger's Personal Finance Magazine* (May 1995), 87.

Chapter 15: Tying a Knot in Your Money: Marriage

1. "Money Talks. We Listened," *Worth,* June 1994, p. 69.
2. Jaine Carter and James D. Carter, "Relationships: Communication Can Pay Off in Fewer Fights About Money," *Holland News Service,* www.detnews.com, July 15, 1997.
3. Gary Smalley, *Making Love Last Forever* (Dallas: Word Publishing, 1996).
4. John Gray, Ph.D., *Men Are from Mars, Women Are from Venus* (New York: HarperCollins, 1992).
5. Dave Ramsey, *More Than Enough* (New York: Viking, 1999), pp. 29, 87–91.
6. John Eldredge, *Wild at Heart* (Nashville, TN: Thomas Nelson, 2001), p. 9.

Chapter 16: Crumb Snatchers and Money

1. Dennis Means, CFP, and U.S. Census Bureau, "Kids Who Return Home," *CNNfn.* www.cnnfn.com, March 31, 2000.
2. "Children Need to Learn Financial Literacy," Bankrate.com, status report cited by Jump Start Coalition, August 16, 2000.

Chapter 17: Family, Friends, and Money

1. Henry Cloud, Ph.D., and John Townsend, Ph.D., *Boundaries* (Grand Rapids, MI: Zondervan Publishing House, 1992), pp. 25, 126, 135–36.

Chapter 19: Why Written?

1. Cindy Hall and Julie Stacey, "Credit scores high at ATM's" and "How often ATM cards are used," USA Snapshots: *USA Today* (n.d.) as cited by the Research Partnerships survey for Cirrus system.

About the Author

Dave Ramsey was born in East Tennessee and raised in Nashville. After receiving a B.S. in finance and real estate at the University of Tennessee, he founded Ramsey Investments, Inc., a real estate brokerage firm specializing in foreclosure and bankruptcy real estate. He is also the founder of the Lampo Group, a consulting firm that offers financial counseling and seminars. During his ten years of counseling and foreclosure brokerage, he has reviewed more than ten thousand foreclosure situations and done in-depth counseling for several thousand families.

During his more than fourteen years of experience as a real estate broker, he has accumulated several titles, and was one of Tennessee's youngest brokers to be admitted to the Graduate Realtors Institute. He has been licensed to sell life, health, and disability insurance and has held mortgage brokers and securities licenses. Dave is currently the host of a popular talk-radio show with hundreds of thousands of listeners daily, called "The Money Game," dealing with financial matters.

By the age of twenty-six, Dave had accumulated over $4 million in real estate. He then lost his entire portfolio and virtually everything he owned. He has now rebuilt his financial life, but that experience combined with years of counseling gives him an unusually deep perspective and insight into money matters, as well as a comprehensive look into the foreclosure and bankruptcy scene.

Dave has been married for over ten years to his wonderful wife, Sharon, and is the proud father of two girls, Denise and Rachel, and one boy, Daniel.